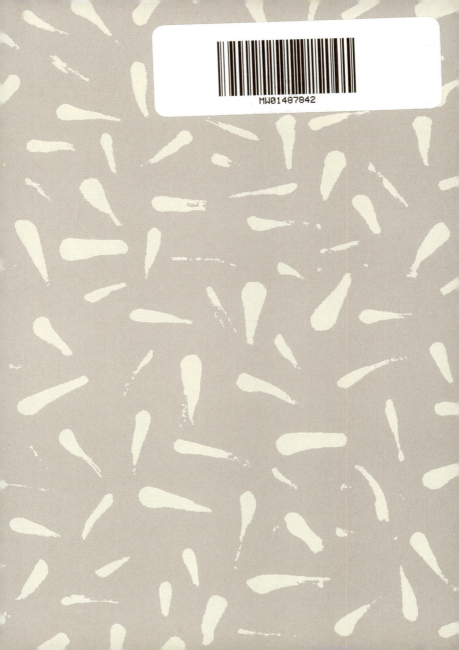

TO _____

FROM _____

DATE _____

GO
FOR
IT

BOLDLY LIVE THE LIFE
GOD CREATED FOR YOU

MELISSA HORVATH

LIVE YOUR FAITH

Go For It: Boldly Live the Life God Created For You
Copyright © 2023 Melissa Horvath. All rights reserved.
First Edition, January 2023

Published by:

21154 Highway 16 East
Siloam Springs, AR 72761
dayspring.com

Unless otherwise indicated, all Scripture quotations are taken
from the ESV Bible® (The Holy Bible, English Standard Version®)
copyright ©2001 by Crossway Bibles, a publishing ministry of Good
News Publishers. Used by permission. All rights reserved.

Scripture quotations marked NIV are taken from THE HOLY BIBLE, NEW
INTERNATIONAL VERSION®, NIV® Copyright © 1973, 1978, 1984, 2011
by Biblica, Inc.® Used by permission. All rights reserved worldwide.

Scripture quotations marked KJV are taken from
the Holy Bible, King James Version.

Scripture quotations marked NLV are taken from the New Life
Version, copyright © 1969 and 2003. Used by permission of Barbour
Publishing, Inc., Uhrichsville, Ohio 44683. All rights reserved.

Scripture quotations marked AMP are taken from the Amplified Bible,
Copyright © 2015 by The Lockman Foundation. Used by permission.

Scripture quotations marked ICB are taken from the International
Children's Bible®. Copyright © 1986, 1988, 1999 by Thomas
Nelson. Used by permission. All rights reserved.

Written and hand lettered by: Melissa Horvath
Design by: Hannah Brinson

Printed in China
Prime: J9581
ISBN: 978-1-64870-906-7

CONTENTS

INTRODUCTION

Hey there!

I'm Melissa—a mom to three little ones, a wife, owner and designer at Sweet Water Decor, and a daughter of the King.

Throughout my life, I have learned to lean on God and not on my own understanding. I've learned to fully trust in His plan for my life and say "yes!" to the callings He has for me. My plans were nothing compared to what He had in store for me, and the same goes for you too!

Do you ever dream up plans for your life and wonder when they'll happen? As humans, we often tend to focus on our own plans and our own timelines, and when our plans don't happen in our own timing, we can shy away from God or think He's forgotten about us when, in reality, the opposite is taking place. Here, He's working *through* it all and *for* us all, for every one of us from the beginning to the end of time— your friends, your neighbors, even those you will never meet. When we start to surrender our plans to His and realize that the plans that God has for us are way better than we can ever imagine, then we can start to live with less stress, knowing that He is taking care of it all for us. His plans may not be exactly what we've dreamed of, but they are a part of His bigger plan not only for us but for everyone else too.

In this devotional, I walk through these everyday topics with you as we learn how to say "yes!" to the callings the Lord has for our lives and surrender the need to be in control. It can be scary to release control, but I'm here with you to share what I've learned as a follower of Jesus about how to lean on Him, relax, and listen!

In my devotional *You Got This*, I wrote about the purpose for your life. And here in *Go For It*, we will explore how to live out that purpose and step deeper into the plans God has for you!

I'm so excited you picked up this book—or maybe you were even gifted it. I can't wait to help you deepen your faith, relax, and start living the life God has created just for you.

I hope you stay encouraged each day! Feel free to follow along and share your new devotional on Instagram and tag me:

@MELISSA_HORVATH_

Cheers!

melissa

HOW ARE YOU?

These things I have spoken to you,
that my joy may be in you,
and that your joy may be full.

JOHN 15:11

It happens every day—maybe when you're chatting with the local coffee shop barista or when you pick up a phone call from a friend—the words "How are you?" are some of the first things you hear. "Good, how are you?" is most likely the answer. But really, how are you? Sometimes we can be hiding hurt and putting on a brave face just to avoid getting into all the nitty-gritty details of what's making us sad. Or it could even be the opposite: we could be on Cloud Nine and having an amazing day, but we don't want to say "Amazing! How are you?" for fear that the other person isn't having a great day and we'll come off as insensitive. Sometimes we can hide our happiness or even fake it.

But no matter the highs or the lows, God wants us to be happy. For some of us, this is hard to grasp through hard days, trials, and more. A good verse to recall is Philippians 4:12–13: "I know how to be brought low, and I know how to abound. In any and every circumstance, I have learned the secret of facing plenty and hunger, abundance and need. I can do all things through him who strengthens me."

The Him spoken of here is Jesus. We can find our strength in Him throughout the day, whether we're having a good day or a not-so-good one. In this devotional, we'll dive deep into how you can rely on His plans for your life so that you can boldly live out the life God has created for you!

The good news is that He's always with you and always ready to hear your prayers. When you are weak, rely on Him to be your strength. When you are joyous, you are allowed to be. It's okay to be happy!

GO FOR IT!

Can you be how you really are? Can you say you're sad when you're sad, amazing when you're very happy, or okay when you're just okay? Accepting how we really are feeling is hard sometimes. Just remember, we've all felt sad, happy, angry . . . and it is totally okay. Jesus wants to be our strength and wants us to be happy! Next time you're asked, "How are you?" try answering honestly! You don't have to go into all the details, but maybe when you ask, "And, how are you?" the other person will be real with you too.

ACCEPTING HIS PLANS

For my thoughts are not your thoughts,
neither are your ways my ways, declares the LORD.
For as the heavens are higher than the earth,
so are my ways higher than your ways
and my thoughts than your thoughts.

ISAIAH 55:8-9

As a follower of Jesus, we're never guaranteed an easy life, an easy path. Everyone has their own struggles and anxieties. It's the learning how to surrender our plans and look to Him in the good times and bad that can get us through it all. We don't have to try to figure it all out alone; we don't have to rely only on ourselves to hold strong through the storms and dark nights. Not every path is a sunny one; that's just not how life is. Sometimes we have to go through the thorns in the dark valleys to come out on the other side. In these times, surrender what you are thinking to God. He will carry you through the storms.

It takes time, but when you learn to rely on Him and not on your own understanding, you can find peace. Just remember, not every destination is a quick one, and He's not just working in your life but in everyone else's too—from the beginning of time to eternity. We have to be patient and rejoice that He has plans that are meant for us. We are living out those plans each day. And rest assured, He's there, even when you can't see Him. Call on Him and receive peace of mind, heart, body, and soul. Our minds can't see like His can, for we're only human. It's okay to be scared or anxious, but He tells us many times not to be. We're reminded of this in Philippians 4:6–7: "Do not be anxious about anything, but in everything by prayer and supplication with thanksgiving let your requests be made known to God. And the peace of God, which surpasses all understanding, will guard your hearts and your minds in Christ Jesus."

GO FOR IT!

When we learn to let God lead our lives and say "yes!" to the callings He has for us and release control, we can start to live in His peace. No matter what you have going on that is stealing your joy, give it to God. Let Him work wonders for you, in His timing.

GOING BACK

Behold, I am doing a new thing;
now it springs forth, do you not perceive it?
I will make a way in the wilderness
and rivers in the desert.

ISAIAH 43:19

Think back to a time when God removed something from your life that needed to change. Did you ever say to yourself afterward, *Maybe I should have stayed with him* or *I should have never left that job* or *Why did I even move away*? Second-guessing—it happens to all of us, right? Whether it was a relationship, job, or a location, as humans we always wonder if we made the right decision. We contemplate and try to put reasoning to it. But when God calls us away from something and puts that nudge in our hearts, we have to listen and obey. Or maybe God wasn't telling us to make a change; maybe it was another person who made the decision for us. We can be left feeling confused and wanting to go back to what feels normal and comfortable, even if it was uncomfortable for us while we were in it. I'm here to tell you, do not go back to something God has already rescued you from because it was "comfortable" or familiar. Don't try to fill that void with what was; instead, fill it with what God has planned for you. Look to Him alone for direction, and thank Him for directing your path, no matter where that may lead. Now, I'm not saying relationships can't ever get back together, but rather focus your heart's desires on those things that God has planned for you. And, if He removed something from your life that was no longer serving you, don't chase after it. When we start living for His plans over our own, we're able to look toward the future with open arms rather than with anxious hearts.

GO FOR IT!

Next time your situation changes, look at what's to come with an open heart and open mind. Know that God is working in and through all things. When you want what *was* back, be reminded that God may have rescued you from it, even things unseen, and be reminded not to undo what He has done. Instead, turn your gaze to Him and decide to rely on His plans alone. Remember, His thoughts are higher than your thoughts. Rest in that peace and trust!

LETTING HIM LEAD

You make known to me the path of life;
in your presence there is fullness of joy;
at your right hand are pleasures forevermore.

PSALM 16:11

D
o you like to be in control? We all do to some extent, and for some of us, it's a constant struggle every day. We can get discouraged when things don't go our way and try to blame others. But what if, instead, we looked at it all as a part of God's plan for us?

Take a deep breath in and out. Ready for some truth? He's the One who is really in charge. We have a free will, but it's His plan that will ultimately win out. He will make known the path of your life step-by-step, in the good times and the bad. Releasing control of our lives is hard, but when we focus our gaze on Him and let Him take us by the hand and lead us on the right path, we can start to live more freely. It's not easy to let someone else lead us, but we can relax knowing that God is the only one we'd want to be having that control!

Be on the alert, as there is an evil presence in this world, and he wants to pull you away from God and deceive you to think your plans are better than God's. This happens more often than you think—even when you're late for a meeting or that plan falls through and you're frustrated, but then God works His good through it all. Your plans weren't His plans.

When you surrender and look to God when the storms come, you'll be prepared. When others don't understand why things happen, you can be that rock that holds strong, knowing that God is in control, and can even share with them this great news. Let come what may, and let yourself rest in the arms of Jesus when you do not understand. Let Him walk with you every day!

GO FOR IT!

Do you ever feel bound by the need to have control in life? Some of us like being in control while others like to be led. But every one of us is on God's path for our lives. When we surrender and let Him lead, we can start to have peace and hold strong, no matter what situation we are facing!

AT YOUR WORST

The LORD is my strength and my shield;
in him my heart trusts, and I am helped;
my heart exults, and with my song
I give thanks to him.

PSALM 28:7

We are all human. We have good days and bad days. There are days when we get mad at situations, yell at those we are close to, and get upset. We cry, we make others cry, and sometimes our days can just spiral out of control. But I'm here to tell you, God still loves you! When these days happen, close your eyes and picture Jesus holding out His hand for you and giving you a hug, letting you know that you are loved! Jesus lived on this same earth you walk on and knows pain and struggle, just like you. Our God is a compassionate God and just wants you to walk with Him. Even on your worst days, when you can't see the light, He is there! All you have to do is call upon Him.

Often we turn to other measures to fill the voids and make us feel better, but the only thing you need is God. Let Him work in and through you! His mercies are new each morning, so stay faithful! Let Him heal your wounds and renew you! Let the pain, anger, sadness . . . all of that and more be replaced with the love He has for you. God sent His only Son to live on earth and die for us all. He loves you, and even if you feel you don't deserve it, you do!

GO FOR IT!

Next time you are at your worst, give yourself grace and call upon the One who is always by your side— Jesus! Know that you are loved no matter what. When you feel things are out of control, instead of trying to fill the void with something else, fill it with the love God has for you. That's what your soul needs!

WORTHY

For you formed my inward parts;
you knitted me together in my mother's womb.
I praise you, for I am fearfully and wonderfully made.
Wonderful are your works; my soul knows it very well.

PSALM 139:13-14

How amazing is it that you're here today? The Scripture from Psalm 139 rings with such truth. God has a plan for you and for your life. You are not here by mistake! You were fearfully and wonderfully made. You have great worth! But when others' opinions creep in, they can make you feel unworthy. It's easy to find your worth in what others think of you or what they say to you. When you let their opinions or words define you, it breaks you down. This is when the negativity and pain creep in, telling you that you aren't worthy of happiness, love, and more.

When you start to hear those negative words creep in, hit the PAUSE button. Your worth shouldn't be found in what others say or think. You are a child of God, born for so many amazing purposes. Don't let others define you. Don't let the worry, the comparison, the mean words break down something perfectly curated from above. We all can have bad days, and cruel critics try to fill voids in their own lives by breaking others down. Remember that they are broken people, and instead of fighting back, choose to pray. Ask God to soften their hearts, and pray that they learn to know Him as you do! Often we can think up false truths in our mind of how others perceive us, fueled by our own insecurities, and the evil one knows what those are and reminds us of them. First Peter 5:8 says, "Be sober-minded; be watchful. Your adversary the devil prowls around like a roaring lion, seeking someone to devour." Know the source, question when these pop up in your mind, and ask yourself if God would really say that about you. In all of these situations, know your worth isn't found in these things but in how God sees you! And He loves you just the way you are. Cling to Him and hold strong, knowing that you are worthy!

GO FOR IT!

Repeat after me: "I am who He says I am. I am a child of God. God has amazing plans for me! I am not what others say or what the negative thoughts say I am, but I am a child of God. He loves me, He knitted me in my mother's womb, and I am loved. I am worthy!"

SEEING THE LIGHT

Again Jesus spoke to them, saying,
"I am the light of the world.
Whoever follows me
will not walk in darkness
but will have the light of life."

JOHN 8:12

Have you ever renovated your home or remodeled your room? I recently went through a home renovation project. Our walls were gray before and now they're white. When friends and family come over, they always remark about how much more sunshine they can see. But the light was always the same, it's just now the visibility is better. This is such a reminder about how God works within us. When our souls are dimmed by burdens, when we try to do life on our own, when we are saddened—it's harder to see the light.

But once we find Jesus and give our worries, our hopes, our dreams to Him and start to lean on Him, our souls are lightened, and that light is visible. It was always there, but it was harder to see! We can start to be that light for others too, and they can see the light within us. When we learn to go for it and trade all those plans we had for His, when we rely not on our own understanding but trust in His, we will become lighter—in mind, heart, and spirit.

When you feel "gray," just be still. Turn from your own understanding and place your hope in Jesus. Just remember, you are never alone. We can often feel that we're the only ones going through what we're going through, but just know that no matter what you're feeling, God is always walking beside you, even when you can't see Him. Place your burdens at the feet of Jesus, and let your load be lifted from you.

GO FOR IT!

We're reminded in John how Jesus is the light of the world. When we choose to follow Him, we don't have to live in darkness anymore. Give it all to Him and begin to walk in the light that He will shine through you! Once you choose to follow Him and God's plans for you, your load will be lighter and others will start to see His light coming from you!

HIS PLANS OVER MINE

*Giving thanks always
and for everything to God the Father
in the name of our Lord Jesus Christ.*

EPHESIANS 5:20

As a child, did you ever desperately want to do something but your parents told you no? They saw what was ahead when you were innocent and didn't know any better. They had your best interest in mind. Think of God as your Father. We want things for our lives, and He says, "Well, I have something better planned for you." We get upset, just as we would at our parents. Sometimes we even turn away from God when what we wanted never happened or hasn't happened yet. Instead, we should be running toward our Creator, the One who knows us the best and has the best plans for us—plans we will never understand fully in this life.

Often we get stuck in our own minds and in our own timelines when we need to let go of control. When we surrender our plans and realize that the plans God has for us are way better than we could ever imagine, we can begin to live stress-free, knowing He is taking care of it all for us! I love talking about this because it has happened so much in my life, and I wish someone had told me these words and I'd given up control years ago. Remember, He's not just looking out for you, He's looking out for all of His children—everyone else out there! He will always be bringing people and situations in and out of your life, for His plan and His glory. He's got you—don't ever forget that!

GO FOR IT!

Today, pray for help to surrender. Pray to have God reveal His plans for your life to you, in His timing. Ask Him for help as you try to not rely on your own understanding but learn to live more freely, knowing that He's making it all happen for you, and everyone else too, according to His plan. Relax and release control today!

LETTING OUR GUARD DOWN

Do not let your adorning be external—the braiding of hair and the putting on of gold jewelry, or the clothing you wear—but let your adorning be the hidden person of the heart with the imperishable beauty of a gentle and quiet spirit, which in God's sight is very precious.

1 PETER 3:3-4

Do you feel like you're living out your true self? Often we can put on a brave face or smile through the pain—while inside, we're feeling much different. We can make our lives look like a highlight reel on social media or like we're living out our untrue selves, just to have others perceive us a certain way. This can even mean going to church each week just to check an imaginary box off our lists. But what are we doing all these different things for?

In these times, we need to give ourselves grace and realize that we don't have to be unreal. We're already loved by Jesus no matter what! There's no box we have to check and no certain way we have to act or be, because we're already known, and we're already loved so much. We can even look at others and wish we were living out their lives, but even those thoughts are a waste of the person we were made to be! It's okay to cry, it's okay to be who we really are.

When we let our guard down and think we have to act, be, or do things a certain way that isn't really true deep down inside, that's where the insecurities come in and evil enters. Those bad thoughts come in, letting us know we're not good enough, and those are all lies we end up believing. Recognize these thoughts as something meant to bring you down and pull you further from God. He wants you to be just who He made you to be—no matter what!

GO FOR IT!

Stand strong in who you are! You were made to be beautiful, wonderful you—not anyone else. You don't have to be something false. When those negative thoughts creep in, know they're not of God; they're meant to bring you down. Dismiss those thoughts and start living who you are!

you were wonderfully made

WALKING ALONE

You, however, are not in the flesh but in the Spirit,
if in fact the Spirit of God dwells in you.
Anyone who does not have the Spirit of Christ
does not belong to him.

ROMANS 8:9

On this path of life, we have ups and downs. Sometimes we can feel that we're walking alone, that no one understands and no one can really know the real us deep down inside—our insecurities, our doubts, our fears, our anxieties. But I'm here to tell you to not fear, because God is with you wherever you go. He goes before you and behind you. He's walking beside you every step of the way. He knew you before you were born, and He will never leave you. Whether in the dark of night or the light of day, you can call upon Him anytime. If you've accepted Jesus as your Lord and Savior, you already have the Holy Spirit dwelling within you.

In John 14:16 (AMP), Jesus describes the Holy Spirit as our "Helper (Comforter, Advocate, Intercessor—Counselor, Strengthener, Standby), to be with you forever." Those nudges you get, those reminders, those callings of your soul, they come from the Holy Spirit. God is not only among us,

He's also within us! How wonderful is that? Sometimes we think we can do it all on our own, but we were never meant to! You have a built-in best friend, right within you and beside you. Take your cares to Him anytime. He's always there to listen, and the best part is, He already knows your heart better than you even know yourself. You may not like the plans He has for you, but if you obey His callings for you and follow His path for your life, they'll be better than you could ever dream up for yourself!

GO FOR IT!

If you haven't accepted Jesus into your heart, when you are ready, invite Him into your life, and the Holy Spirit will begin to live inside of you too! If you've already done so, focus on knowing He's always there for you, no matter what. Set it all at His feet and thank Him for all that He's done for you—the seen and unseen. Call upon Him anytime you need; He's always there beside you and within you!

IDOLS

You shall have no other gods before me.
You shall not make for yourself a carved image,
or any likeness of anything that is in heaven above,
or that is in the earth beneath,
or that is in the water under the earth.
You shall not bow down to them or serve them,
for I the LORD your God am a jealous God,
visiting the iniquity of the fathers on the children
to the third and the fourth generation of those who hate me.

EXODUS 20:3-5

U sually we think of idols as statues; we don't often think of them as social media, sports, our friends, or something or someone that we're putting above God. Sometimes we can get caught up in life and forget to put God first. We can find ourselves mindlessly scrolling through social media or being involved in something that takes so much attention that we end up setting it to a "god" status in our lives. When our focus turns away from God, that is when the idol attraction increases. We cannot serve two masters. We see this written in Matthew 6:24: "No one can serve two masters, for either he will hate the one and love the other, or he will be devoted to the one and despise the other. You cannot serve God and money."

Sometimes we can end up worshipping the created thing over the Creator. What are the idols in your life? It's scary to think about sometimes, as often these can be great things God has given to us. An easy one can be our phones. Take a look at your screen time this past week, and it may shock you! Give yourself grace. We're all imperfect beings, and we're not meant to be perfect. But if we start to learn about what's taking our focus off of what God wants for us and putting it on other things, we need a little reminder to not make those things idols in our lives.

GO FOR IT!

What are you putting above God? It can even be a good thing that ends up turning into a god-like thing to you. Start to think about what those are and see what you can do to lessen the impact they have on your life. Today, pray about those things and how you can better serve our one true God.

PURSUIT

Behold, I stand at the door and knock.
If anyone hears my voice and opens the door,
I will come in to him and eat with him, and he with me.

REVELATION 3:20

Do you like to set goals or just see what happens? Some days can seem the same as the next, and we can often get into a rut. Many of us have both long-term and short-term goals. But today I want to ask you: What is your pursuit in life? Is it what you want for your life, or did you ever think of it as what God wants for your life? We often think of pursuing work or family goals, but what about our relationship with Jesus and God's plans for us? This is a heavy question to ask ourselves, and it can be hard to know the answer. First and foremost, make it a pursuit to have a relationship with Jesus, not just religion. Going to church and believing is one thing, but when we learn to walk with Him and trust in Him, our relationship can grow into trust and surrender.

Let me ask you: What is keeping you from your relationship with Jesus and having faith? Believe it or not, God is pursuing you! He wants to have a relationship with you too. Second is surrendering your plans for His. It's very important to have that trust in God and live out His plans for your life. It's hard to not have control, and it's scary to pursue what He puts on your heart that may be out of your comfort zone. But when you do, just wait. Wonderful things will happen that are all a part of His larger plan!

GO FOR IT!

Today, think about your faith in Jesus and your pursuit of Him. The best thing is that He loves you just the way you are, and He wants a relationship with you that is deeper than just going to church. He wants you to trust and lean on Him through it all! If you're unsure how to take these next steps, just pray. Have faith in the Lord and surrender. Like any relationship, it takes time, and He can't wait to have this time with you!

BELIEVING AND RECEIVING

And I tell you,
everyone who acknowledges me before men,
the Son of Man also will acknowledge
before the angels of God,
but the one who denies me before men
will be denied before the angels of God.

LUKE 12:8-9

Believing in God is a beautiful thing. It means to trust and have faith in Him. However, believing doesn't always equal receiving all the things we want. Having a relationship with Jesus, going to church, and praying doesn't mean that life will be easy and all of our desires will be fulfilled. This is a hard concept for some to grasp, as we feel that if we do all the right things, God will give us our heart's desires. Really, it's more about saying yes to the desires He has for us rather than those we have for ourselves.

We can look at others who don't have faith and how great their lives look and feel like that isn't fair. But we're not seeing the whole picture. Do they really have it all, without a relationship with Jesus? It is tempting to put worth in possessions when we our worth is in Jesus.

When God doesn't answer prayers the way we want, we can find encouragement by looking around us for the blessings He *has* given us. There are so many that we will never even see—things we never had to think about because He's saved us from them!

GO FOR IT!

Next time you pray, try to remember that God already knows your desires, even before you ask. He has your and everyone else's best interests in mind. If things don't turn out as you would have hoped, have faith and be still, knowing that He's got this!

FINDING JOY

Count it all joy, my brothers,
when you meet trials of various kinds.

JAMES 1:2

Occasionally I start off having a great day. The sun is shining, things are going well, and then suddenly something goes wrong. The stress and anxiety take over, and the joy seems to fade. Even the smallest event can turn my day upside down. I am trying to learn to acknowledge it, give it to God, and move past it so that I can still live in joy.

We're not meant to let anyone or anything steal our joy. Often, when our circumstances are upsetting, we start to dwell on the negative rather than on the joy we can receive through Christ—the joy that was His plan all along.

Check out what it says in Nehemiah 8:10: "Then he said to them, 'Go your way. Eat the fat and drink sweet wine and send portions to anyone who has nothing ready, for this day is holy to our Lord. And do not be grieved, for the joy of the LORD is your strength.'" This verse helps me remember that through the Lord, I can receive strength to overcome any obstacle!

We're reminded in James 1:2 to count it all joy when we meet trials. We usually look at trials as negative things, and we can let them upset us, but I am discovering that sometimes joy can be disguised in trials I face.

Today, let's look for the joy—even if that's simply knowing that it's all in God's hands and it's all a part of His greater plan!

GO FOR IT!

Don't let anyone or anything steal your joy! The Lord is your strength. When you go through terrible times and your soul sinks, you can find joy in the Lord. Praise Him even in difficult circumstances, for He has all understanding, and we only have limited human understanding. Next time you face a trial, count it all as joy.

THE GLORY

*For from him and through him
and to him are all things.
To him be glory forever. Amen.*

ROMANS 11:36

When I think back to my school years or even times at work as an adult, I can remember doing a project only to have someone else take all the credit. It felt so much better when someone noticed my hard work and told me I'd done a good job.

We always have a choice about who we give the glory to. Often we credit ourselves for our successes, but it helps to remember Who it was that got us to where we needed to be. A good saying is "Not I, but through Christ in me." When we live in a posture of working hard yet staying humble—and remembering the One Who got us there—we do so not for our own pride but for His glory!

Sometimes we see this when watching football, when a player gets a touchdown and points upward, thanking God for what God did through him. When we think about the talents and gifts we've been given, when we help others with our gifts or do something great, let's remember Who that all came from and give credit where it's due. Without those God-given gifts, we wouldn't have been able to accomplish what we did or help others.

At the end of the day, it's all for His glory! He loves seeing us use what we've been given, and I'm sure it brings Him great joy!

GO FOR IT!

Next time you receive a pat on the back, give the glory to God and see how the other person reacts. You can give honor to God even in the smallest circumstances. But don't just say it! Believe it and know it! What are some gifts God has given to you that you can take out into the world and use to His glory? Remember, all good things are from Him and for Him!

TRUSTING BLINDLY

*Jesus said to him, "Have you believed
because you have seen me?
Blessed are those who have not seen
and yet have believed."*

JOHN 20:29

As a kid, were you ever blindfolded and led by someone to pin a tail on the donkey or hit a piñata? We had to trust blindly where the other person was leading us so we could win some candy or place that tail just right. Having faith is similar to this in that we follow and trust a God we've never actually seen. How can we trust without seeing? Relying on faith over sight is hard! We have to trust, blindly.

This happens especially when we're in a storm and can't see past what's in front of us. We have to call upon the One who can calm the seas to guide us. That's why it's good to have strong roots. Think of a tree with shallow roots. When a storm comes, it topples over. If we deepen our relationship with the Lord and learn to grow deep roots, then we can stand firm when the storms come, trusting blindly that He will get us through. Our branches may fall, but we will stand strong and firm, grounded in His Word and His love for us.

GO FOR IT!

You don't want to prepare for a storm when it's too late. If you've ever watched the news during hurricane season, you've seen people boarding up their homes and businesses, buying water, and putting out sandbags. They prepare for the worst before the storm hits. You can think about this in regard to your relationship with Jesus. Spend time with Him so that He can strengthen your faith before the storms hit hard in your life, then when they do, you can endure them. Others will see how you've weathered the storms, and you can share your faith with them so that they may find Jesus too!

DOING WORK WITH LOVE

Whatever you do, work heartily,
as for the Lord and not for men,
knowing that from the Lord you will
receive the inheritance as your reward.
You are serving the Lord Christ.

COLOSSIANS 3:23-24

Out of all of the many chores I do each week, I hate making the bed with fresh sheets the most. I always feel like I can't ever get the fitted sheet on just right, and tucking in the top sheet is just not my forte. I was doing this the other day, and God reminded me to do work (even the stuff I hate to do) with love. I know my husband appreciates it when the covers are tucked in well, even if it's something I'm not the best at.

I think we can all relate to this scenario one way or another. Maybe for some of us it's doing the dishes, or the laundry, or washing our cars. Instead of thinking of how much we hate doing what we're doing, we can think instead of how much it will help us or someone else. This is great practice even at work when we're given a task that we just want to keep putting off. How can we actively do the work we need to do, whether it is at home or at work, with love? Sometimes we'll never know how the work that we're doing can impact others. I love the reminder in Colossians (read the verse at the top of this devotion) that we're not just doing work for ourselves—we're serving Jesus.

Today, let's remember the saying "service with a smile" and actually practice doing our work with genuine happiness. I can't wait to see the difference it makes!

GO FOR IT!

I encourage you to think of how you can serve not only yourself but others too, by doing work, chores, and tasks with love. How can you go above and beyond today and serve others—and most importantly Jesus— through your works? See how you can find the joy of doing something out of love this week and see how it changes the way you view the work you have to do!

PRAYER AND FAITH

Rejoice in the Lord always; again I will say, rejoice.
Let your reasonableness be known to everyone.
The Lord is at hand; do not be anxious about anything,
but in everything by prayer and supplication
with thanksgiving let your requests be made known to God.
And the peace of God, which surpasses all understanding,
will guard your hearts and your minds in Christ Jesus.

PHILIPPIANS 4:4-7

Have you ever noticed that when you pray, a lot of times your focus can turn toward what you need for that particular day? It's so easy to let our gaze wander away from so many blessings we are given, and become consumed with what we need fixed or adjusted. And then, if God doesn't fix or adjust it right away, we can get anxious. We cling to our worries instead of giving them to God. Why should we hang on to what God already has a hold of? Is there something holding us back from truly being able to lay our burdens and prayers at the feet of Jesus? Do we created beings feel that we know the best outcome more than the Creator does? These are all great things to remember when we feel we know what's best for us and pray with that expectation. When we go to God in prayer, we can fully give our concerns to Him.

Let's intentionally remember our blessings, even if it's food on the table and a roof over our heads. When we let our focus shift to gratitude, we can find confidence that our concerns are never too big for God. We're reminded in Colossians 4:2 to be thankful for how He answers our prayers, no matter what: "Continue steadfastly in prayer, being watchful in it with thanksgiving."

As our faith grows, we start to rely on His answers to our prayers. We read about the miracles that happened in Bible times but we forget that He's still performing miracles today, many that we'll never even know about!

GO FOR IT!

As you go to God in prayer, believe and know He hears you, and place everything at His feet. As your Father, He wants to hear from you! The outcome may not always be what you want, but remember, nothing is ever impossible for God! Today, come to God with what's on your heart. Then, remember the blessings He's already given you, no matter how small!

unanswered
prayers
means
God had
something
better
planned

CHOOSING GRATITUDE OVER CHAOS

Fear not, for I am with you; be not dismayed,
for I am your God; I will strengthen you, I will help you,
I will uphold you with my righteous right hand.

ISAIAH 41:10

I t can be easy to start our day discouraged. We can have a thousand things running through our minds—endless to-do lists and constant errands here and there—and let those stresses take over the happy moments going on all around us. We often put our focus on what's bothering us or what needs accomplishing that day, and we miss soaking in all the blessings.

Sometimes I can feel unsettled until a few things are crossed off my list for the day, which can make me feel defeated before the day has hardly begun. I can let these discouraging moments have a lot of power over me, causing anxiety. Instead, I want to remember that God does not want me to fear, and that He is here to help me.

Next time we start to feel anxious about all that we have to accomplish, let's remember that chances are, what's bothering us right now will be a memory in a few days.

God tells us He will strengthen us and help us—even through those times. When we take time to regain focus on the good things, we can push away stress and worry and replace them with positive thoughts. One way we can do this is to think of some things that we're grateful for. In a season of chaos, our blessings may be hard to see through all the debris, but there is always something good, even if it is simply the sunshine peeking through the clouds or clean water to drink. It may be small, and that's okay. It will help us shift our focus away from what's swirling around us. The things causing us stress in this moment will not last forever.

GO FOR IT!

Today, focus on the good and find some blessings between the chaos and worry. God wants you to focus on the good, and He has promised to strengthen and help you. He doesn't want you to be dismayed. What are you grateful for that you can be reminded of in times of chaos? What helps you to regain calm in these times?

PRACTICE

Trust in the LORD with all your heart,
and do not lean on your own understanding.

PROVERBS 3:5

When we are in the waiting, it can be hard. We wonder, "Will that job, spouse, kids, house . . . life ever come?" We want what we want right now, in our own timing. We forget that what's best for us is often yet to come. But what if we changed how we thought? What if we pushed back on what we wanted and focused instead on trusting what God wants for our lives? The wait may never result in what we want but what we need instead.

We tend to forget that God is working behind the scenes in ways we cannot see or understand not only for you and me but for everyone else as well throughout the span of time. And don't get me wrong, waiting is hard, but on the other side of it is God's plan, which is always greater than our own! When I was a teenager, I wanted to find my husband in high school, but God had different plans. Then, when I went to college, I searched for him there— and again, God had different plans. I had to develop a trust that there was a better plan than what I had in mind. And maybe my husband was supposed to find me, not the other way around. We have to release that control and learn to rely on our faith in God over our own fear of the unknown so we can stay the course. We may never understand or see it, but it's best that way. Our knowledge is limited, and His is vast. He sees what we can't and knows what is best.

It may take years, months, or the longest minutes ever, but no matter what, God's timing is best. There is still beauty in times of waiting. Let's soak up all that we can.

GO FOR IT!

Next time your patience is running thin and you're wondering when something will happen, just enjoy the season you are in and know that God is working through it all—even through your frustrations. He wants you to be patient and rely on Him and not on your own understanding. So soak up everything you can while you're in this season. And above all, trust!

YOU ARE STRONG AND COURAGEOUS

Have I not commanded you? Be strong and courageous.
Do not be frightened, and do not be dismayed,
for the LORD your God is with you wherever you go.

JOSHUA 1:9

It's comforting to know that God is with us wherever we go. Sometimes we can feel that we're alone or that He's left us, but truly He's by our side always! We need strength and courage in our daily lives in order to boldly live out the plans God has for us. Of course, there are seasons of life that require more strength and courage than others. So how do we do this? Strength means more than just physical ability; we can be strong in our faith too. As we grow deeper in our faith with the Lord, we can trust in Him more. It is comforting to know He's by our side and that we can call upon Him at any time. Just as consistent physical exercise builds muscle, we grow stronger in faith when we practice relying on God for our needs. Often when we face trials we can stray from God, when we should be moving toward Him instead.

Sometimes we need courage when God calls us out of our comfort zone to live boldly for Him. There are moments when we feel prompted to do something out of the blue, maybe talk to someone or pay for someone's drink in the line ahead of us or smile at a stranger. These are promptings from the His Spirit within us to share God's love with others.

This can go even deeper when we have a strong urging from God to make a big life change such as move to a different city or start a new job. We can't take these proddings lightly. One courageous step could lead to amazing things. I'm sure we can all think of a situation in our lives when acting on a prompting from God has led us to something great. That took courage!

GO FOR IT!

Next time a positive nudge comes up, act on it. Live boldly in these moments because they can be from the Lord, even if it's something small like buying the drink for the car ahead of you in line at a coffee shop. You could make that person's day when they need it the most. How do you feel about being strong and courageous, and how can you show others how to be as well? Maybe through your acts, you can help others be bold and do the same!

RELEASING CONTROL

For I know the plans I have for you,
declares the LORD, plans for welfare and not for evil,
to give you a future and a hope.

JEREMIAH 29:11

Who else likes to be in control? (Raising my hand here!) Whether it's control of our own situations—keeping us from harm, stress, disease, heartbreak, or even controlling the TV remote—we all have times when we feel as if we can handle life on our own. But what if we just released it? That's a scary thought, right?

What happens when we try to control the uncontrollable? One of these moments for me came when I got Covid-19. For two years I'd avoided so much, worn my mask everywhere, wiped down my groceries (and even had them delivered to my home). I was afraid, so I tried to control as much as I could in order to not get sick.

One of the bigger ways I altered my life because of Covid-19 was changing my plans for when to grow our family. In 2020, my husband and I wanted to try to get pregnant, but we decided to wait because of all the uncertainty that came with the pandemic.

Fast forward to January 2022: I was twenty weeks pregnant, and two days after I got my booster shot, I got Covid-19. Scared, pregnant, and sick, it felt as if my world was crashing down around me as I cried to the doctor in the ER. Since I'd been so careful, I wondered how I got it. But, ultimately, I had to relinquish control to God. It was scary, but my faith had to take over the my fear.

We get the ability to choose in life, but God's plans reign over all. Since God sees the past, present, and future, and things we can't see, we can rest in Him, trusting that He knows what is best. Sometimes we have to accept the plan He has for our lives, even when we don't like it. God is able to take whatever comes our way and transform it for our good. When we rest in this truth, we are better able to trust in Him in the moments when life spins out of control. Along the way, our faith roots grow a little stronger and we are freed from a life of fear.

GO FOR IT!

Today, I challenge you to release control, no matter what that looks like. This could be over something as simple as the desire for the perfect day or the perfect dinner, or even the perfect life. Let God lead you, and surrender control to Him!

YOUR NEW YEAR

What then shall we say to these things?
If God is for us, who can be against us?

ROMANS 8:31

The ball drops and it's finally the new year! This is the time when everyone jumps on their New Year's resolutions. But, let's be honest, sometimes those commitments only last a few weeks or so until life returns to normal.

We often associate the new year with change, but we can start over any day, at any time. We can start on a new path at the end of February, or even make our "New Year's resolutions" in the middle of June. We don't have to wait until January to start something new.

It's hard for those of us who like to have our "ducks in a row" to change plans in the middle of them. Just know that we don't have to continue on a path that's not working out for us just because we have already started down it and invested time in it. I often like to reference a "sunk cost" when describing these situations because it's a cost that has already been incurred and can't be recovered. We don't have to continue in unhealthy relationships, jobs, or anything else just because we have already invested in them. Time and resources that have been already "spent" can't be recovered.

I started my "new year" when God led me to quit my full-time job and pursue running my own business. If that's not a leap of faith, I don't know what is! I had to let my faith take over and be strong and courageous to boldly live out His plans for me.

It's never too late to change our lives and follow God's plans for us. It may happen out of the blue or it may be years in the making, but when we're called to start our "new year," we may have to switch up our own plans to boldly make the choice to follow those God has for us.

GO FOR IT!

You can begin your new year at any time. Whether you're getting nudges from God or you want to try something new, just go for it! It may take you out of your comfort zone, but don't let it be a new year's resolution that only lasts a few weeks. If you jump in the waters, commit to swimming to the other side.

GIVE YOURSELF GRACE

He said to me, "My grace is sufficient for you,
for my power is made perfect in weakness."
Therefore I will boast all the more gladly of my weaknesses,
so that the power of Christ may rest upon me.
For the sake of Christ, then, I am content with weaknesses,
insults, hardships, persecutions, and calamities.
For when I am weak, then I am strong.

II CORINTHIANS 12:9-10

We make mistakes, we get upset at ourselves, we "mess up" because, well, we're human. We're imperfect beings living in a sinful world, surrounded by imperfect beings. It is easy to let society shape our thoughts, desires, and actions. We might look back on the times when we did something we're not proud of and allow those memories to haunt us. Our shame might even cause us to feel unworthy of the love God has for us.

The great news is that no matter how much we mess up, God still loves us! It might help to give ourselves some grace and remind ourselves of the truth in God's Word. Psalm 37:23–24 is an especially comforting passage during the times when we have made mistakes. The psalmist writes, "The steps of a man are established by the LORD, when he delights in his way; though he fall, he shall not be cast headlong, for the LORD upholds his hand."

We all mess up. Those who came before us faced the same struggles, and those who came after us will too. God wants to help us get back on track when we make mistakes.

We are children of God, and just as parents love their children, He loves us, even more than we can imagine. He wants us to keep our focus on Him and His love, no matter what. Just as a child needs her parents' love and support even as an adult, we always need God's grace. Our worth isn't in what we've done—our worth is in Jesus, who already died for our sins.

GO FOR IT!

Where do you need to give yourself grace? Nothing is too big to bring to God to ask for forgiveness. But you also have to forgive yourself. God wants you to bring your mistakes, especially those that haunt you, to Him in prayer. Just remember I John 1:9: "If we confess our sins, he is faithful and just to forgive us our sins and to cleanse us from all unrighteousness." Facing your failings may be tough, but you can find peace in God's grace. God loves hearing from His children (you!), and there's nothing you can say that He doesn't already know. And just remember, He loves and cares for you!

PRAYING FOR OTHERS

*Therefore, confess your sins to one another
and pray for one another, that you may be healed.
The prayer of a righteous person
has great power as it is working.*

JAMES 5:16

Every once in a while, I find myself praying and thinking mostly of myself. It's easy to do, especially when we know what we'd like or need. Others may ask us to pray for them, or we tell them we'll pray for them when we hear of a not-so-great situation, but sometimes it's hard to remember to pray for them beyond that moment when we tell them we will.

When we think about boldly living out the life God created for us, we think about ourselves, but our lives are full of so many people. What if we pray for others too? This may look different for everyone. The girl who has yet to find her soulmate might pray for her future husband and in-laws. Another person might pray for a future boss to help lead her well. Someone else might pray for their child's teacher in school, or a friend, spouse, parent, or even for a stranger who passes by.

Whatever the case, coming to God in prayer for others is what we're called to do—including praying for our enemies.

Let's think about what Jesus had to say about this issue in Matthew 5:44: "But I say to you, Love your enemies and pray for those who persecute you." This one is tough to do. It is human nature to feel that those who have harmed us in some way are unworthy of our prayers. Jesus teaches us to look at it differently, to understand that grace is never about how much we deserve. It is always a gift.

GO FOR IT!

Who is in need of prayer today? You could choose different people each day, really thinking about what they need and bringing those needs to the Lord. Also, try to think of some "enemies" you can pray for—genuinely. Maybe it's someone from your past whom you haven't forgiven yet, or someone who cut in the line in front of you today. You may not know what they need, but God does!

CHANGING PERSPECTIVE

Not that I am speaking of being in need,
for I have learned in whatever situation I am to be content.
I know how to be brought low, and I know how to abound.
In any and every circumstance, I have learned the secret
of facing plenty and hunger, abundance and need.
I can do all things through him who strengthens me.

PHILIPPIANS 4:11-13

Occasionally, I need to do a self-check and ask myself some hard questions: Do I like to be right? Do I have a hard time hearing other people's opinions? Do I prefer my own ideas and ways over others'?

It can be really helpful to learn to listen to the thoughts, plans, and opinions of others. We might not even realize how often we ignore others' ideas or get upset when our own aren't used. We might not realize how others feel when we push our ideas on them. This can happen in so many ways—whether it's what we decide on for dinner with our families, or what to accomplish in a meeting at work, or even following God's plan over our own.

It makes a huge difference when we put ourselves in someone else's shoes and try to see from their point of view. One of the best ways to do this is to really listen. We can often be quick to think only of our own side of the situation rather than what others want or need. It might feel good when our ideas are accepted, but how does the other person feel?

In a similar way, we can get upset when God's plans for our lives are different than ours. What if we tried to see the situation from God's perspective? God is the author of our lives, and He knows our story from cover to cover. We can trust in Him when we don't understand, realizing that He does. The Creator of the universe knows more than our human minds can comprehend. He is faithful in all things!

GO FOR IT!

Whether it's a small decision like where to eat out for dinner or a larger life decision, it helps to make room for others' thoughts and ideas. Try to release the need for control and let someone else pick what to do, where to go, and more. Take time for a perspective check. Is it possible to see their side?

The same goes for trusting in God. Release that control and try to remember that His perspective is much grander than your own. You might find that the next time another's idea or plan wins out, you are happy to go along for the ride!

QUIET TIME

I have calmed and quieted my soul,
like a weaned child with its mother;
like a weaned child is my soul within me.

PSALM 131:2

I rarely get time to myself. In the midst of work and home life, I find the moments to just be still are few and far between. Sometimes we need time to get re-grounded. Whether it's because of a stressful day, the felt need to remove ourselves from the chaos around us or simply to pray, it helps to find a quiet spot to regroup. We can even find this when there is busyness around us. Washing dishes can let us focus on one task, calming our hearts and souls. Taking a shower can give us the opportunity to renew our minds as we close our eyes and listen to the water fall around us. We might even try imagining Jesus washing away any pain, worry, or shame down the drain. In these moments, we can ask for forgiveness or intentionally open our hearts to receive God's love for us. I often find that it's during these quiet times that I hear ideas from God or little reminders of things to do.

We can find a quiet spot in our homes or at the local coffee shop, build a campfire, or spend time in nature. For those of us who live near water, maybe it's sitting by the beach or listening to the river or putting our feet in the lake. It doesn't matter what our personal retreats look like as long as we make space to still our minds and hearts so that we might rest in God's love.

GO FOR IT!

We all need quiet time to restore our souls, in addition to sleeping of course. Where can you find rest and relaxation, even if it's only for a few moments each day? Does it involve water, being out in nature, or a cozy spot in your home? What do you need to come to God with today during this time to truly restore your soul? Today, I encourage you to spend some time in this spot or try out a new one.

Let God renew you today!

VICTORY OVER STRONGHOLDS

For though we walk in the flesh,
we are not waging war according to the flesh.
For the weapons of our warfare are not of the flesh
but have divine power to destroy strongholds.
We destroy arguments and every lofty opinion
raised against the knowledge of God,
and take every thought captive to obey Christ.

II CORINTHIANS 10:3-5

What is a stronghold? I think of a stronghold as an attitude or mindset that has a grip on us—a weakness, something we have a negative attitude about, an unhealthy habit, or something we struggle with. We often keep these secret instead of bringing them out into the light.

Strongholds can vary greatly and can even include things we thought were okay—like overindulging in food. Other examples can include, but of course are not limited to, obsessive worry, jealousy, or selfishness. Maybe we know the root cause of our stronghold, or maybe we don't.

When we acknowledge that we have a stronghold in our lives, we can face it honestly and begin to break free from it. Some strongholds, however, are too powerful to shake alone. In these circumstances, it helps to find someone we can confide in. This person or group can be an accountability partner for us, and maybe they can even share with us the strongholds they struggle with too. When we feel the stronghold coming on, we can reach out to them for encouragement. Knowing that we have someone in our corner can be very helpful as we take on this fight. The battle is often spiritual, which means we need God's help to break free. It's written in II Corinthians 10:4: "For the weapons of our warfare are not of the flesh but have divine power to destroy strongholds."

It might help to think of Jesus' character and ask ourselves, *Would He do what I am falling into?* When we feel drawn into the stronghold, we can ask God for help and try to shift our focus onto something else. Even just taking some deep breaths and walking away can make all the difference.

GO FOR IT!

What is something that has a stronghold over you? Some of us have many. The first step is acknowledgment. Think, *What did this stem from?* Is it stemming from a desire to be accepted or to prove worth and value? Is it stemming from a need for more love and attention? Or something else? Remember, your value and worth are not determined by others but by God, who loves and accepts you for who He's created you to be—you!

BEING PURSUED IN THE PAIN

In the fourth watch of the night he came to them,
walking on the sea. But when the disciples saw him
walking on the sea, they were terrified, and said,
"It is a ghost!" and they cried out in fear.
But immediately Jesus spoke to them,
saying, "Take heart; it is I. Do not be afraid."
And Peter answered him, "Lord, if it is you,
command me to come to you on the water."
He said, "Come." So Peter got out of the boat
and walked on the water and came to Jesus.
But when he saw the wind, he was afraid,
and beginning to sink he cried out, "Lord, save me."
Jesus immediately reached out his hand
and took hold of him, saying to him,
"O you of little faith, why did you doubt?"

MATTHEW 14:25-31

We will all experience hardship, pain, and sadness throughout life—it's inevitable. We wonder why things happen, and sometimes we'll never know. In these times, we can stray from God or think He's punishing or abandoning us. We might quit going to church or praying. We might get angry and think He's against us and not for us.

When pain draws near, what if we ran toward God rather than away? God loves us and wants us to trust in Him in all circumstances. We can cling to Him.

Rather than thinking God is punishing us, we can remember that He's pursuing us. He heals us, comforts us, and guides us. When Peter and his friends were on a boat one night, they ran into trouble because a strong wind was against them. The Bible tells us that as they were struggling, Jesus walked across the water to reach them. Peter asked Jesus to allow him to walk across the water too, and Jesus granted his request. Then Peter got really scared. He started to focus on what was happening around him, and as he did, he began to sink. When he cried out to Jesus for help, Jesus reached out and caught him. As He did, He reminded Peter to have faith.

When difficult times come our way and we find ourselves afraid, let's remember Peter's story and keep our focus on Jesus, instead of what's happening around us.

GO FOR IT!

Today, try keeping your focus on Jesus and His love. Remember, Jesus is pursuing you! Let Him into your heart to change and grow your faith. Don't stare at the storm; look to Jesus instead.

ENJOY DOING WHAT YOU LOVE

Oh give thanks to the LORD,
for he is good;
for his steadfast love endures forever!

PSALM 118:1

The things that bring us joy are as unique as we are. Some of us love watching the sunset, others enjoy being with friends or family, painting, running, or going on a bike ride. We can let life pass us by and forget to do the things we love. There's always something else that is claiming our attention, and it can be tempting to put ourselves on the back burner while we take care of others, work, and life.

Today, let's block off some time on our calendars to do what brings us joy. Maybe we can wake up early to watch the sun rise, or instead of scrolling through social media on our lunch breaks we can take a walk. It's pretty great that each and every one of us enjoys something different.

Time keeps moving along. If we aren't intentional about making space for what brings us joy, our days will slip by without that happening. What if we plan to make time for doing what we love more regularly? It might just change our lives.

GO FOR IT!

Think about what makes you happy and what you really enjoy doing. Give thanks to God for making you just the way you are, and pencil in some time on your calendar to make sure you do something just for you! It's hard not to feel guilty for taking that time, but we all need to enjoy doing something we love to bring joy to our souls!

STAYING CONTENT

Godliness with contentment is great gain,
for we brought nothing into the world,
and we cannot take anything out of the world.
But if we have food and clothing,
with these we will be content.
But those who desire to be rich fall into temptation,
into a snare, into many senseless and harmful desires
that plunge people into ruin and destruction.

I TIMOTHY 6:6-9

We live in a world where we're constantly bombarded by what is the next "must-have" item—whether we see it in a commercial, on social media, or even at our neighbor's house. Maybe it's not even a thing. It could be a relationship, our appearance, or our social status. It is easy to fall into the trap of wondering why others have something different than us. In these times, it's hard to stay content with what we have when we're wishing to have something more.

Can contentment bring happiness? Let's take a look back and think of something we have today that we prayed for in the past. It can even be as simple as having a great friend to confide in. Once God gave us what we desired, did we forget about how much we wanted it?

The good news is that there is no shame in being content with where we are in life. One of the great things about trusting in the Lord is seeing what He has in store for us. Instead of constantly wanting something different, we can enjoy the wonders He has for us!

Often with my small business, people ask me, "What's next?" or "What is your goal?" Since I was a business major in college, my response should be something financial, but I tend to surprise people when I say, "We'll see what God does next!" I've had this mentality since I started Sweet Water Decor, and He's made things happen I could only dream of. Sometimes we can set the bar really high for ourselves and fall short. If we just see what God has in store for us instead, we can be surprised by what He does for us rather than be upset about the things that didn't happen.

GO FOR IT!

Today, say a prayer of thanksgiving for what you already have. Ask God to help you stay content with what He's provided for you. Thank Him for all He's given you. Be reminded today that it's perfectly okay to be content where you are and see what God has in store for you.

STOPPING THE OVERFLOW

*Come to Me, all you who are weary and burdened,
and I will give you rest.*

MATTHEW 11:28 NIV

A t work, one of the things I design is a soap dispenser, and I love having them at our sinks. Recently, I was refilling one, and God prompted me to stop well before I got to the fill line. Then He gave me the visual of how I sometimes "overfill" my life. It was a beautiful picture of how we can say "yes" to too much in life. It is possible to fill our lives with so many activities and life happenings that we have no room left for anything else. When we do this, we push ourselves to the brink, without leaving room for ourselves, relaxation, or to simply be.

We live in a fast-paced world, and we often say yes to things just to keep others happy, even if it costs us our own happiness. Instead of filling up our entire glass, perhaps we could try leaving some room so that we can be sure not to overfill. When filling my soap dispensers, there have been many times I've thought that I had just a little more room. Then when I stuck the pump back in, there went all the soap, all down the sides of the bottle. When we do this with life, we can get anxious, feel rushed, and stress out ourselves and even our families. Let's think about how we want to fill our own "dispensers" in the time we have each day.

GO FOR IT!

Do you ever feel like you are being overfilled with things to do, responsibilities, and commitments? For what do you wish you had a little more time? One of the things we often push to the back burner is time with God. Today, I challenge you to look at all you have to do and where you are saying yes when you should be saying no. Ask yourself where you can make some time for other things in your life.

SCRIPTURE AND PEACE

Peace I leave with you; my peace I give to you.
Not as the world gives do I give to you.
Let not your hearts be troubled, neither let them be afraid.

JOHN 14:27

All of us have days when nothing seems to go right. Wouldn't it be nice to just jet off to a beach during these times? Sadly, for most of us this isn't a reality, but we can develop our own coping mechanisms to find rest, solace, peace.

In today's Scripture reading, Jesus tells His disciples that true peace comes from Him. This is such a good reminder. While we can find temporary peace in earthly things, situations, and places, Jesus offers us lasting peace.

It's good for us to have a plan for the next time we feel anxiety creeping in. One of the things I do in these moments is play Christian music on my radio or home device. Some people love new worship songs, while others find peace in hymns. Singing these words can remind us that God is here for us, and that we can release our problems to Him.

Another way to bring calm to your day is to repeat and memorize a passage of Scripture. One of my favorite verses to call upon when I'm having a rough day is Jeremiah 29:11: "For I know the plans I have for you, declares the LORD, plans for welfare and not for evil, to give you a future and a hope." Scripture can remind us that God has a plan for us, and that we can trust Him to love and care for us.

GO FOR IT!

Do you have a favorite verse of Scripture that helps bring you peace? It's good to begin thinking about what can calm you before hard times come. Whether it's turning on Christian music or remembering a Bible verse, God wants to show you that He can bring a peace that lasts.

GO WITH IT

Seek the LORD and his strength;
seek his presence continually!

1 CHRONICLES 16:11

There have been times when I've started down a path and found myself wanting to quit, only to realize that I had no choice but to keep moving forward. I remember going on a hike in college through the gorge near campus with a few girls who lived in the same hall as me. As we were hiking, we decided to go down a steep hill to get near the water. It was a beautiful place deep down in the gorge, and we kept hiking along the water. We went pretty far before we realized that we had to climb back up a very steep hill to get back to campus. Equipped with just my tennis shoes, I needed God's strength to keep going as I put my hands on roots sticking out and in mysterious holes (wondering what might come out of them) to climb back up to higher ground. Afterward, I wished that I hadn't gone, even though we saw some amazing views. It gives me chills thinking about it to this day, but thankfully we all made it back to the top.

Sometimes we just have to keep going, even when we can't see what's next. I think this happens for a lot of us when we're in the valleys of life—when we don't know what's next. In these times, we have to rely on God to see us through even if we don't know what next steps to take or how long it will take to get back up to "higher ground."

There are some of us who are waiting to hear from God or waiting to see the next steps in our lives. Whatever the case, we can find strength in God to help us stay the course. No matter what direction we're headed, Jesus will guide us and walk with us along the way.

GO FOR IT!

As the peaks and valleys come, remember to take one step at a time, depending on Jesus for guidance and strength. There will be times when you just have to push through, but know you're not walking alone. Jesus is always near. When you're afraid, call on Him.

BEING HAPPY FOR OTHERS

Rejoice with those who rejoice,
weep with those who weep.

ROMANS 12:15

When we hear good news from friends, family, or even a stranger on social media, are we happy for them? Or do we think of our own situations and find ourselves feeling a bit resentful of them? Let's be honest, we've all gotten stuck in the comparison trap at one point or another. How can we truly be happy with those who are rejoicing?

In Romans 12:15, we're reminded to rejoice with those who rejoice and weep with those who weep. We can each have our time in the sunshine. Realizing that God has more than enough blessings to go around frees us to be genuinely happy for others when things are going their way.

The above verse is a good reminder to be there for those who are weeping as well. We all need someone to lean on sometimes. John 11:33–35 tells us that when Jesus witnessed His friends Mary and Martha grieving over the death of their brother, Lazarus, He wept.

Jesus had compassion for Mary and Martha when they were hurting, and we can follow suit. Whether it is rejoicing or weeping, it is good to have true and honest compassion and connection with others.

GO FOR IT!

As humans, we need each other. God's love empowers us to shift our focus from our own situations to be truly happy for others when things are going well for them. When we trust that God has enough blessings to go around, it is easier to wait patiently for our own time to shine.

HOW GOD SEES YOU

Therefore, if anyone is in Christ,
he is a new creation.
The old has passed away;
behold, the new has come.

II CORINTHIANS 5:17

There are some of us who struggle to feel worthy of God's love. Maybe we've made mistakes that left us feeling ashamed or even unworthy to talk to Him. Or maybe we go to church each week but are unsure of how to have a true, deep relationship with Him.

The wonderful truth is, God sees each of us through the eyes of love.

Like a loving father, God wants us to have a relationship with Him. In Ephesians 1:4 we learn that "even as he chose us in him before the foundation of the world, that we should be holy and blameless before him." God sees each of us as holy and blameless, through Christ. In John 1:12–13 we learn: "But to all who did receive him, who believed in his name, he gave the right to become children of God, who were born, not of blood nor of the will of the flesh nor of the will of man, but of God."

No matter our past or present, we are welcomed to have a relationship with the Lord. We don't ever need to feel unworthy of coming to Him, as He has always been pursuing us, throughout our whole lives.

GO FOR IT!

Where are you in your relationship with God? Have you ever felt unworthy of His love for you or unsure of how He sees you? Read over the Scriptures mentioned in this devotion for a reminder of how loved you really are!

you were born for this

BE GENTLE WITH YOURSELF

No one ever hated his own flesh,
but nourishes and cherishes it,
just as Christ does the church.

EPHESIANS 5:29

We can be so hard on ourselves. Those of us who are moms might experience "mom guilt." There are others of us who are hard on ourselves concerning how often we are exercising and have a negative image of our bodies. The ways we criticize ourselves are endless and hurtful.

One of the greatest things is, God made each of us unique, with special talents, and there will never be anyone else like us. We are all made beautiful, just the way we are—inside and out! When we shame ourselves, we shame what God has made. That's pretty hard to swallow, right? It is difficult to treat ourselves with kindness when we focus on how we compare with others. Let's try focusing on how God sees us instead.

GO FOR IT!

What are you really good at? What makes you feel beautiful? What's an accomplishment that you are proud of? Today, thank God for these things and ask Him to help you see yourself the way He sees you: beautiful, precious, and loved. Just as you are.

SILENT VERSUS ABSENT

Before they call I will answer;
while they are yet speaking I will hear.

ISAIAH 65:24

Sometimes we can confuse silence with absence—especially when it feels like we are not hearing from God. It might even feel like He has forgotten about us.

Silence never means that God is not working. He always is. It is comforting to remember that it's all in His timing, not ours. We want answers right now, but there is beauty in practicing patience. We can learn to trust in God and rest in the fact that He's working everything out behind the scenes. He's always with us.

Even unanswered prayers can be confused with absence. We may never see or know the reasons why our prayers weren't answered in the ways we asked, but many times that is a blessing. There are things we are meant to know now and things that are kept from our knowledge for a reason. Isaiah 55:8–9 reminds us that the way God thinks is very different from the way we think: "For my thoughts are not your thoughts, neither are your ways my ways, declares the LORD. For as the heavens are higher than the earth, so are my ways higher than your ways and my thoughts than your thoughts."

We can be confident that God hears our prayers, and just because they aren't answered in the time we need them to be or how we want them to be doesn't mean that He doesn't have our best interest in mind.

GO FOR IT!

What prayers are you waiting on answers for now? Have you heard from God, or is He silent? Just know His silence doesn't mean that He's forgotten about you. It may take days, months, or even years to see what the outcome will be, but never lose faith in Him!

PRAY AND REJOICE

Praise the LORD! Oh give thanks to the LORD,
for he is good, for his steadfast love endures forever!
Who can utter the mighty deeds of the LORD,
or declare all his praise?

PSALM 106:1-2

Do we come to God only with our problems? God loves to hear our prayers of praise and gratitude as well. We can become so focused on the problems we want Him to fix for us and others that they consume us. It is easy to take the good things God does for us for granted. What does our prayer life look like? Do we send up praise to Him even when times are difficult? Do we thank Him for something as simple as having food to eat today or making it to work on time when we thought we'd be late?

God wants to hear from us in all things. Praise flows naturally when we pause to remember that all blessings flow from Him. At church when I was growing up, we'd often say the Doxology written by Thomas Ken: "Praise God from whom all blessings flow; praise Him, all creatures here below. Praise Him above ye heavenly host. Praise Father, Son, and Holy Ghost. Amen."

How about praising God during the storms of life? This practice will help us grow in our faith, making it easier to lean on Him as new storms arise, because we have learned that He knows what's best!

Whatever our situations are today, we can pray confidently, knowing our words will be heard. Let's keep our eyes on Jesus. He's got this!

GO FOR IT!

Do you pray with no strings attached? During your prayer time today, think about a few things for which you can offer either thanksgiving or praise. Next, what storms can you pray about and tell God you'll trust Him through? Last, bring your needs and the needs of others to Him in prayer. How will it change your prayer life now that you know you can pray through it all?

WHO HE IS

"I am the Alpha and the Omega,
the first and the last,
the beginning and the end."

REVELATION 22:13

I'm sure each of us has family members or friends who don't believe in God. Sometimes this happens because when they were children, people of authority failed to show them an accurate picture of who God is, leaving them unsure about His character.

Or, maybe past hurts in their lives have made it difficult for them to trust, and because of that, they are unsure of how to have a relationship with Him.

Let's take a moment to consider a few of the things Scripture says about God's character. In John 8:12 Jesus said this about Himself: "I am the light of the world. Whoever follows me will not walk in darkness, but will have the light of life." There are times when life seems really dark, and we don't know what to do next. Because of Jesus, we won't walk in darkness but will have the light of life. He is there to lead us through hardships. He'll be beside us, no matter what.

First John 4:8 says this about God: "Anyone who does not love does not know God, because God is love." God doesn't just love us. He *is* love.

What about Psalm 34:8, which proclaims, "Oh, taste and see that the LORD is good! Or Isaiah 44:6, which teaches us that God is eternal? "Thus says the LORD, the King of Israel and his Redeemer, the LORD of hosts: "I am the first and I am the last; besides me there is no god."

Our God is eternal. He is love. He is light. And He is good!

GO FOR IT!

How can these truths about God help replace any negative feelings toward Him that you have? How can you help others to see the light in the darkness and process any pain they feel toward God? In I John 5 we're reminded that in Him there is no darkness at all. Today, don't forget that. Let's refocus and remember who He is!

LEAVING THE PAST THERE

Remember not the former things,
nor consider the things of old.

ISAIAH 43:18

Sometimes we find ourselves with regrets about our past, but we need to leave them there. God loves us and wants us to give ourselves grace. He wants us to live in the present rather than in the past. We all make mistakes. Thankfully, God can redeem it all. He restores the mess, hurt, pain, tears, and more. Even though we may not have been aware of Him, He has always been by our sides. We can trust in the plan of the God who loves us! Let's remember what we learned earlier—He is for us and He is still good, even in the hard times.

The past is best left there, in the past. We can't change it. I know people in my life that bring up the past a lot and question why things happened the way they did. They have let those situations bother them not just for days but for years, decades even. Instead of trying to wrack our own brains to understand, we can trust that because God loves us there will be brighter days ahead.

GO FOR IT!

Stop trying to figure it all out yourself. Don't let the hurt of the past continue to bother you today. Instead, focus on God's love for you. God knows our hearts and what each of us needs, and today, trust in that rather than your own understanding of any situation.

BE A BLESSING

It is God who works in you,
both to will and to work for his good pleasure.

PHILIPPIANS 2:13

It's pretty amazing that each and every one of us is unique. God thought us up even before we were born, to be a part of this world for His glory! He's given some of us the gift of hospitality, others serving, others compassion, others to be great at art, others math, and all combinations in between. My daughter is really good at making sure others are taken care of, and she's only three. She always wants to help me with whatever I'm doing, whether it's putting clothes away or making sure everyone is fed or cleaning. My five-year-old son is a thinker. He's always looking out for his sister and for ways to fix things that are broken as he thinks through situations and what's connected to what. I can see the blessings God gives others through them even though they are so young!

I'm here to remind all of us that we, too, have amazing gifts. One way to figure out what our gifts are is to think about what comes naturally to us. What gifts do we have to offer this world as a blessing to others? We all need each other in this life. If everyone was the same, it wouldn't work well, and God knew that!

God loves seeing His children using their gifts for His glory and for His good pleasure. Using these gifts may come so naturally to us that they don't even seem like work. What about our families and friends—what gifts can we see that they have been given, and how are they using them well? How can we help them be a blessing to others too?

GO FOR IT!

We each have talents and gifts to use as a blessing for others. Often we can be hard on ourselves rather than celebrate ourselves. Today, focus on what makes you, you! Think of your friends and family as well. Encourage them to use their gifts to be a blessing too. A simple text, phone call, or note to let them know what good you notice in them might make their day. Let's celebrate one another and what God has given each of us, for His glory!

PRAYING IN THE STORM

Ask, and it will be given to you;
seek, and you will find;
knock, and it will be pened to you.

MATTHEW 7:7

Whenever I think about how difficult it is when we feel as if our prayers are unheard, I always go back to the season when I was waiting for my husband. I prayed for a husband for many years and wondered if my prayers would be answered. Eventually, I decided to go ahead and start building my life as I waited. I decided to buy a townhouse, and a few days after closing, I had my first date with the man who turned out to be my husband. My husband didn't pop up when I expected him to but when God wanted him to. This is such a good reminder for those who are praying for something, to trust in God's timing. God knows our hearts and our wishes, and He is working in and through all things to piece everything together according to His plans. It's best not to rush into things just because we're impatient. It's better to wait for God's best.

God hears our prayers! Let's keep praying, even through the pain and confusion. We don't have to let the difficult wait ruin our lives. Instead, we can go ahead and live fully while we wait. It's all about trusting and having faith when we pray, not about what we want but what He has for us.

A part of that is accepting that what we are asking for may never come to pass. This is very tough to do, and we may never understand it. But through it all, we can be confident that there is a bigger picture out there that none of us can see or understand—but God does.

GO FOR IT!

Waiting in prayer is difficult. When you're in those prayerful, confusion-filled, and hopeful days, keep the faith and be patient. Place your trust in God and not on your own understanding. Remember, He is a loving God, and He knows what's best for us, even when we don't know just yet!

YOUR WILL, YOUR WAY

Not everyone who says to me, "Lord, Lord,"
will enter the kingdom of heaven,
but the one who does the will
of my Father who is in heaven.

MATTHEW 7:21

Too often we stay in places or do things that we know aren't the best for us. We get that pit in our stomach or nudge in our soul that we need to make a move to change situations or relationships. In God's timing, He makes a way, and we have to follow. I remember being in an old job and knowing it wasn't where I was supposed to be. God prompted me to check out a new workplace, and I acted. He moved me away from the anxiety and pain I was experiencing in my old job to somewhere I needed to be, just when I needed to be there.

Sometimes we have to be uncomfortable for a while until God paves the way for us. When we know it's time to make a move in our lives, no matter what that looks like, it is best to act and not delay.

We can become so used to things that we ignore the calling to move on. Instead, we get stuck in an unhealthy situation when we know we should move away from it. We are reminded in Matthew 7:21 to do the will of God and act when He says "go!"

One short prayer to remember is this: *Lord, if it's not Your will, take me away from it.* But it's up to us to act. He won't physically remove you (probably), but He will continue to prompt you to make the change when He knows it is best.

No matter what, just surrender and obey and, most importantly, act when the timing arises.

GO FOR IT!

Have you ever felt uncomfortable and known it was time to leave a relationship, situation, or job? Did you hear from God to move on? The pit we can feel in our stomach is there for a reason, and His timing will prove when it's right to change situations. Pray to know when it is the right time to move, and when it is, don't delay.

SPREAD JOY

A joyful heart is good medicine,
but a crushed spirit dries up the bones.

PROVERBS 17:22

One of my favorite things is when someone ahead of me in line at the coffee shop pays for my drink. It's a simple little joy that keeps spreading as I then pay for the car behind me and it keeps on going.

Often on bad days we live with a cloud over our heads, and it's hard to see any joy in the day. When we are feeling down, sometimes it helps to try to spread some joy to others. The example above is simple, but it feels great when we know we have made someone's day through a random act of kindness.

We have two choices: We can either look at a situation as one that can bring joy, or we can do the opposite. On those days that we feel our joy has been taken away, let's challenge each other to spread joy to others instead. Simple acts of kindness can go a long way. Even if it's hard to smile, we can give a smile to a stranger anyway, or let a car go in front of us. There are plenty of different ways to spread some joy to others. Their joy can be what brings us joy!

And on the days when we are having a good day, let's multiply it to others! We could say "hello!" to an old friend with a phone call or send some surprise snail mail (aka an actual card!) to a loved one with a gift card for some ice cream, or even spend some extra time in prayer for them.

GO FOR IT!

Proverbs 17:22 says that a joyful heart is good medicine. How can you spread some joy to others today? Bringing some joy to others can bring joy to your own heart too. Let's have some goodness today!

It's a
great day
to have a
great day

FINDING COMMUNITY

Let us consider how to stir up
one another to love and good works,
not neglecting to meet together,
as is the habit of some,
but encouraging one another,
and all the more as you see
the Day drawing near.

HEBREWS 10:24-25

When we are in school, we almost always have people around us who are like-minded. Maybe they also love art or really enjoy math, just like we do. We form friend groups of those we can relate to and confide in. But as we get older, finding time with friends can be more challenging.

When I graduated from school, I joined my church's women's small group. This was the first time I was ever part of a Bible study group. I was surrounded by women I didn't know, ones who were in their twenties and thirties, most not married or with kids yet, like me. We studied different parts of the Bible throughout the years and grew to become friends. Our shared interest in finding community was the only connection we all had. Now, over ten years later, I still see these women at church. Many of them are married and have kids. It's neat how we've been able to be there for each other over the years.

God calls us to meet together with others. We're not meant to live alone. As humans, we need connection, whether we realize it or not. Just the other night, I went on a shopping trip alone and stopped at a local fast food place to get something quick to eat. It was dark out, and as I sat in the parking lot eating my dinner, I looked around and saw other people sitting in their cars too. Then I noticed the glow of their phones. They were all there by themselves yet needed to feel connected.

GO FOR IT!

It is so important to find a community through which we can help lift each other up, open up to one another, and provide support. We aren't meant to live life alone. Are you a part of any groups today? Take a look at those offered in the community or at your church or another local church. You'd be surprised how many others are also needing community!

HAVING ENDURANCE

Therefore, since we are surrounded by
so great a cloud of witnesses,
let us also lay aside every weight,
and sin which clings so closely,
and let us run with endurance
the race that is set before us, looking to Jesus,
the founder and perfecter of our faith,
who for the joy that was set before him
endured the cross, despising the shame,
and is seated at the right hand of the throne of God.

HEBREWS 12:1-2

When I was in junior high school, I ran cross country. The other runners and I would train so that we could run for miles on end and still finish well. High school runners, who were older and more experienced than us, ran with us to help teach us. No matter the weather, we'd have meets with other schools. Even on the days it was snowing, raining, or extremely hot, we had to keep running, not only for ourselves but for our school. When we saw the finish line, we had to keep pushing forward, maybe even faster, to pass runners from other schools and help our team gain points.

In our faith walk, we must have endurance too. We train, going through trials, valleys, and storms, and with each trial, we learn to rely on God more. We run with others—finding community, going to church, sharing our faith, and praying—which helps grow our relationships with God. We have lots of races throughout life, and we have to keep going, relying on our faith to get us through all kinds of obstacles—through the storms, rain, sunshine. We have to put forth our best effort even when we feel like falling or quitting.

Others who are more experienced can run with us to help us build our faith. Finding a faith-filled friend to counsel us may be just what we need to give us encouragement and support.

When we focus on the finish line—being with Jesus forever in paradise—and keep our eyes on Him through it all, we can push through adversity and know God's plans for us are best. Then, as we become stronger in our faith, we can run with others, helping them build their endurance too.

GO FOR IT!

Are you in it for the long haul? Having endurance can be hard, but as we run this race of life, we need more than just training and support. We have to rely on God and keep our focus on Jesus through it all.

ACTIVE WORSHIP

God is spirit, and those who worship
him must worship in spirit and truth.

JOHN 4:24

Growing up, I went through the motions when I went to church. Each week was pretty similar, and I didn't feel anything deep in my spirit when we'd sing hymns for the worship part of our service. When I was a teen, I got my first study Bible from church when I had confirmation. Each day before bed, I'd flip to a random page, and it was just what I needed to hear to get me through those teenage years. It wasn't until college that my roommates and I found a different church where my spirit was truly moved during worship. We sang songs that I understood the words to, and I was moved.

This is when I discovered active worship versus going through the motions. We learn in John 4:24 that we must worship in spirit and in truth. Now, this looks different for everyone. My extended family loves the hymns; they run deep in their souls and bring them joy in worship. But I needed something different.

Where I attend church now, worship is half of the service time. We sing many songs even before getting into the message. Sometimes, as we worship, it can be easy to allow our minds to begin to wander, but what if we really focused on the Lord? Picturing Jesus as I worship makes so much of a difference for me—it helps me to worship in spirit and truth, making worship more meaningful. For my husband, it's different. He focuses on the words that are being sung and the truth behind them. We see others around us who worship in all other kinds of ways. They might lift their hands or hold them in front of them, as if to extend their worship to the One above.

No matter what our preference is in worship, we are all called to worship in spirit and in truth. Some people have never worshipped before and aren't sure what that's like. Others are the way I was growing up, going to church but just going through the motions. When we find the right church home for us, however, we know. It feels different than it ever has before, a place where we feel comfortable and experience the presence of God.

GO FOR IT!

What does worship look like for you? What helps you remain focused on God during that time? It is hard to block out distractions and keep your attention on God, but when you do, you're doing what we're called to do—to worship in spirit and in truth!

HE'S MAKING MOVES

Jesus said to them,
"My Father is always at his work
to this very day, and I too am working."

JOHN 5:17 NIV

Sometimes I am so in awe of modern technology! We put dishes in the dishwasher, and it washes them for us. And the same with a washer and dryer for our clothes— we just put what's dirty in, wait a little bit, and out come clean clothes! During that time, we get to do other things, trusting the machine is doing its job.

That is nothing compared to what happens with Jesus. He never stops working on our behalf. He is working when we're doing other things and when we're sleeping. He was even working for us before we were born. Isn't that wonderful?

He makes a way when there seems to be no way. What's even more miraculous is that He's working for *everyone*, from the beginning to the end of time, piecing it all together like an intricate puzzle. Sometimes we can be wrapped up in our own heads and think only of ourselves, but there's a much bigger picture that God is painting that we are all a part of.

We're called to come to Him in prayer always, and He will hear us. For example:

> And this is the confidence that we have toward him, that if we ask anything according to his will he hears us. And if we know that he hears us in whatever we ask, we know that we have the requests that we have asked of him (1 John 5:14–15).

> "Then you will call upon me and come and pray to me, and I will hear you" (Jeremiah 29:12).

Let's keep praying and have faith! God hears our prayers, and He is working on our behalf. He's making moves around the clock for us!

GO FOR IT!

Isn't it amazing that God is working in our midst and behind the scenes? Sometimes you might want to know how it'll work out, but just stay in constant prayer and have faith that God hears your prayers. Often it can be better to not know how it all works— that's where faith comes in.

ALWAYS THE SAME

*Jesus Christ is the same yesterday
and today and forever.*

HEBREWS 13:8

Raise your hand if you are searching for something constant in your life. Some of us have had friends come and go, or issues in our family. Others have gone from job to job or have had to move many different times.

What a relief to know that Jesus is a constant in our lives. We learned in Hebrews 13:8 that He is the same yesterday as He is today and will be forevermore. He didn't come to this earth in a beautiful palace but in a stable and in a manger. During His ministry, He went to those in need, those whom others wouldn't even want to go near or touch, and He healed them. During His life on earth, He showed care, compassion, and love to everyone around Him.

That same Jesus is always present in your life. He cares for you! He loves you! He desires to have you follow Him and have a relationship with Him. He wants you to cast all of your cares upon Him, so that you can be freed of these burdens. He is the Prince of Peace.

As this life can be unpredictable and things come and

go, one thing remains the same—Jesus. Houses, jobs, relationships, and friends may come and go, but we can trust Him to be there for us through it all.

The Word of God also stands the test of time and lasts forever. Take time to ponder this beautiful verse in Isaiah 40:8: "The grass withers, the flower fades, but the word of our God will stand forever." As other things let us down, fade, or go away, we can rely on this truth to bring us peace and stability in our lives.

GO FOR IT!

Are you seeking something that can be constant in your life? It's reassuring that it can be Jesus. Today, come to Him in prayer thanking Him for His words in the Bible that were true thousands of years ago and are also true today and will be true forevermore.

WATCHING YOUR WORDS

There is one whose rash words are like sword thrusts,
but the tongue of the wise brings healing.

PROVERBS 12:18

It's interesting and helpful to see how Jesus spoke to others in the Bible. He spoke truth and love. That's not always easy for us to do. People can upset us, and we can say hurtful things to them. Proverbs 12:18 tells us harsh, rash words can deeply wound others. We can make people feel pretty terrible and not realize how our words can pierce like a sword, even when that wasn't our intention.

Many of us have had someone say something to us that hurt like that. It is a terrible feeling. Unfortunately, we have all been the one saying the hurtful things. When it is all over, we often wish we could take it back or maybe say it a different way. How can we live more like Jesus and be wise to bring truth and love to the situation rather than harsh, rash words?

There's a TV show that my kids really enjoy watching, and it talks about what to do when you get mad: Before you do anything, take a breath and count to four. This is a good practice for adults too. We can take a breath, remove ourselves from the situation, and give it some time before we respond to others. Not every situation can end peacefully. We are humans, and understanding one another isn't always easy. But we can make the decision to speak wisely versus harshly.

Leviticus 19:18 paints a good picture for us to remember: "You shall not take vengeance or bear a grudge against the sons of your own people, but you shall love your neighbor as yourself: I am the LORD."

GO FOR IT!

How can we be loving toward one another instead of hurtful? I love I Corinthians 13:4–7. It reminds us what love looks like: "Love is patient and kind; love does not envy or boast; it is not arrogant or rude. It does not insist on its own way; it is not irritable or resentful; it does not rejoice at wrongdoing but rejoices with the truth. Love bears all things, believes all things, hopes all things, endures all things."

Keep this as a good reminder to pause before sending that angry message or take a break before saying harsh words. Think of how you can show others love first and be wise rather than rash.

DUCKS IN A ROW

May the God of peace...equip you with everything good
that you may do his will, working in us
that which is pleasing in his sight, through Jesus Christ,
to whom be glory forever and ever. Amen.

HEBREWS 13:20-21

My husband and I knew pretty quickly after we started dating that we wanted to be together forever. After over a year of dating, we decided to look for engagement rings. Little did I know he purchased the ring immediately after we looked. Fast forward about six months, and he popped the question. I never knew he had the ring hidden in his closet for half a year before he proposed until after we were engaged. He waited because he wanted to have all of his "ducks in a row." He was studying for the CPA exam, as he was in accounting, and he wanted to wait until he passed all of the tests before we got engaged. Turns out, he ended up passing the last one after we got engaged.

Sometimes we feel like we need to have our ducks in a row before we make the next step in our lives. We say things like: "After my vacation . . . " or "After I get that promotion . . . " or even "Once I buy a house, I'll do this or that."

When we're called to do something, we don't have to wait for things to be perfect to get started! We can trust that the Lord has equipped us with what we need in the moment to make the next move.

Sometimes we don't feel ready yet and want to wait until we get more things accomplished before getting started. As I write this, I think of my business, Sweet Water Decor. I had no idea how to ship items or even have a business plan in place before starting my shop, but I learned along the way, and God equipped me in each area as I needed to learn it. If I had waited until I "knew it all," I think I'd still be waiting on what He was calling me to do years after I was called.

GO FOR IT!

What are you waiting to start or do until you have your ducks in a row? Maybe you can recall something from your past, or maybe you have yet to come across this time in your life. It can even be simple things like starting a garden or starting that home renovation project—it doesn't have to be a big life change. When God calls you to move, move! He will equip you along the way, so don't delay!

THE EASY WAY

Everyone who goes on ahead and does not abide in the teaching of Christ, does not have God. Whoever abides in the teaching has both the Father and the Son.

II JOHN 1:9

Some of us prefer to take the easy, well-known path. Others are more on the wild side and choose the path less traveled. One person may like each day to follow the same routine, while another tries to make sure each day is always different.

We often associate living the easy way of life with staying in our comfort zone. It's predictable with less worry. Even in those times when we're called to change, we stay right in our little bubble.

But what if we did something new, something different? What if we got out of our comfort zones? There are those of us who have wanted to pursue something different for years, but were scared of what others would think about it. Others hesitate to make changes because they think they don't have it in them to do it. I love seeing the videos on social media of women who decide to renovate a part of their house themselves, defying the stereotypes that accompany women and that type of work. It's something these women always say—that they broke out of their comfort zone and tried something new, something they could be proud of, and found an untapped talent that they developed along the way.

Sometimes God gives us those little nudges, but we tell Him no. We make up excuses as to why we shouldn't do what He's calling us to do, and we miss out on all of the amazing and beautiful new plans He thought up for us. Instead, we could go where our hearts are leading and listen for that guidance. What if we quit talking ourselves out of what He has in store for us, get out of our comfort zones, and go for it?

GO FOR IT!

Do you ever think that you have a secret talent that's untapped that God has given you? If you stay in your comfort zone, you may never know what that could be. Maybe you're afraid to do something alone, but you may be missing out on something wonderful that you may love! When you step out of your bubble, don't be afraid of failure. It could happen, but what if you never tried?

Where in your everyday life can you take it a step further or in a different direction? Are you being called to do something but are too scared to do it? If you're getting that gut feeling to go in that direction, move! God will direct your path. Don't be afraid of what good can come when you step out and try something new!

LIVING IN THE SUNSHINE

Casting all your anxieties on him,
because he cares for you.

1 PETER 5:7

Every time I go outside for a walk and the sun starts to peek through the trees, I just close my eyes and soak it all in. I was picking up my son from school the other day, and another mom caught me with my eyes closed as I faced the sun. She said, "I should do that too!" and closed her eyes and turned her face toward the sun. It was a colder day, and living in Pennsylvania, those days when the sun is shining are a blessing. For some reason, when the sun is shining, it brings not only wonderful warmth but happiness too.

This helps remind me to "live in the sunshine." Let's release our worry and cares to the One above! We can soak up the sun and know God has us in His hands, no matter what we're going through. God doesn't want us to worry our lives away. He wants us to trust in Him and His plans for us, over our own.

First Peter 5:7 reminds us to cast our anxieties on God. We can live in the warmth of His love because He cares for us!

GO FOR IT!

Today, find the sunshine no matter what you're going through, and let joy fill your soul, knowing God's got you! And don't forget to occasionally turn your face toward the sun, eyes closed, soaking up this wonderful gift of light and warmth that God has given us.

radiate positivity

BEING YOU

For we are his workmanship,
created in Christ Jesus for good works,
which God prepared beforehand,
that we should walk in them.

EPHESIANS 2:10

We are God's workmanship! Wow, those are some powerful words right there. We were created for good works as well, and that's amazing—to know we were created for special purposes, which God prepared before we were born.

Occasionally, I will see someone on TV or social media who isn't afraid to just be who they are. They are just themselves, unapologetically. They don't worry about facing criticism because they are exactly who God created them to be. It is so inspiring.

What about us? Are we afraid of being ourselves, exactly how God made us? Do we hesitate to show who we are on the inside because we are afraid of the judgment of others? Sometimes we even assume what others think of us, and this causes us to not be who we truly are. We were made to do good works—but not all works. We don't have to be good at everything, but tapping into what talents and abilities we do have and simply living out who we are is wonderful.

God, the Creator of the universe, has created each of us and has a plan for our lives! That's pretty amazing. When we start to feel bad, ashamed, or unforgivable, we can take a moment to remember how special we are and how we were created for good works!

GO FOR IT!

How amazing it is that you are you! We can be hard on ourselves, but God wants us to be free to be who we really are and live out the good purposes He has created us for. How can you best live out who you are? Today, say a prayer to thank God for who He created you to be and ask for Him to help you live that out each day!

LIVING OUT TODAY

This is the day that the LORD has made;
let us rejoice and be glad in it.

PSALM 118:24

How can we really go for it with a positive attitude and vision each day? Psalm 118 reminds us that each day is a gift and a reason for joy. Read it again and again, and let it sink in. This day is for the Lord. That is a great reason to rejoice and be glad. It's also a beautiful reminder to let Him guide us throughout each day.

We have no idea how big the universe is, but when we look up at the stars, it helps us realize how small we are in comparison to everything else. I recently saw a video that compares the size of our planet and sun to other planets and suns in the universe, and they are so small in comparison to some giants out there. Remembering this helps me put my problems in perspective and remember how "small" they are. How amazing it is that we live on a planet that can sustain life. We have air to breathe and water to drink— just realizing these things can help us rejoice in this day no matter what happens. There's so much to be thankful for outside of our own lives, dreams, and worries.

We're all given twenty-four hours in a day—how do we spend them? Whether we're at school, at work, or with kids, or some combination of all, we can be a reflection of the Lord in all we do. Can we forgive others, speak kindly, and bring joy to others? Each day is a fresh chance to show God's love, and that is a reason to rejoice!

GO FOR IT!

Today, let's end the devotion with a prayer: *Lord, I want to surrender my thoughts, anxieties, and goals to You. You have created me to do good works. Lord, I know You have a plan to see me through today and help me make the best choices I can. Let all of my works glorify You and Your kingdom. Amen.*

PRAISE THE LORD

Do not be conformed to this world,
but be transformed by the renewal of your mind,
that by testing you may discern what is the will of God,
what is good and acceptable and perfect.

ROMANS 12:2

My daughter is in preschool as I write this book. Recently, she shared a prayer with us at dinner that they say during lunch at school: "Thank You, God, for lunch today. One, two, three…Praise the Lord!"

She says it with such enthusiasm that we have her say it each night before dinner. She and our oldest son take turns, or they say it together. But what will happen when they go to elementary school if they pray before a meal like this? They might never do it in fear of what others would think of them. It's not always easy to boldly live out our faith and love of our Lord.

How can we stand up for our faith in a society that doesn't often accept it? It can be taboo to talk about our faith to others outside of church settings. Sharing my faith on social media through posts, and even on the products I design, has been a freeing breakthrough for me.

Even for those of us who are not yet ready to share our faith, that may change in time. When we get to the place we are more comfortable sharing about Jesus, what are some ways we can help spread the good news of His love? It doesn't need to be as bold as sharing our faith in the grocery store aisle, but if we look around us, I am sure we could find someone who needs encouragement or a helping hand.

GO FOR IT!

How can you have that childlike faith and boldly live it out and share it with others? So many people are afraid and don't want to share their faith, but what if there is someone out there who needs to hear it today? You never know who you are helping, so don't be afraid!

OVERFLOW

*In the same way, let your light shine before others,
so that they may see your good works and give glory
to your Father who is in heaven.*

MATTHEW 5:16

In college I finally found a church that I felt at home in, a church that served my soul. They sang an original song about God's love overflowing. It was the first time I was truly moved by worship music, and every time I'd sing it, I would cry.

What really moved me about the song was the idea of filling up our cups so full of God's love that we can overflow, so that it spills out onto others. God wants each of us to experience the fullness of His love and help others come into relationship with Him. As we spread our faith to others, their cups will start to become filled too until they overflow on to others, and faith begins to spread.

We can use our brokenness, our valleys, and our scars-to-victory stories to help bring others to Jesus. Sometimes we might be too scared to open up, but the hard times we go through can help others go through them too—to know there is a breakthrough on the other side, and that begins with Jesus.

Instead of filling our cups with doubt, worry, or anxiety, let's fill it with God's love. As others see us unshaken, they too may draw near to having a relationship with God.

GO FOR IT!

Find a worship song today that moves your spirit and spend time singing and praising His name from the rooftops. And don't be scared to cry! Fill up on all His goodness. And ask Him how you can be a blessing to others. Maybe you're not there yet, and that's okay too. Today, be reminded that God is always with you wherever you go.

SPRING CLEANING

As we look not to the things that are seen
but to the things that are unseen.
For the things that are seen are transient,
but the things that are unseen are eternal.

II CORINTHIANS 4:18

We just went through a home renovation, and it gave us the chance to purge a lot of our "clutter." Those items were no longer serving us, so we donated them or gave them away to friends and family. I think it's hard for some of us to give up "things" as we can place a lot of value and worth in treasured possessions. As I give things away, I always think that if I'm not using them, I know someone else can and they may be needing them. I can't tell you how many times I've posted something to give away and someone sent me a message saying it was just what they were looking for! I think God is working in these moments, and it's pretty great.

Just as we give away what's "cluttering" our homes, God does this for us at times in relationships, jobs . . . and much more. Sometimes when that happens, we can't understand why and can even get upset, frustrated, sad, or angry.

There have been times in my life when I wondered why

relationships would end, and now I can see that God was working through it all. Now, as I look back, I can see it as a blessing.

We can hang on to a lot of "clutter" in our lives that can take up space in our hearts, minds, and souls. When something is no longer serving us, we can let it go to make room for what's meant to be for us instead.

GO FOR IT!

What clutter do you have in your life that you need to part with? It can be items lying around your house, or even something cluttering your mind that you need to give to God. When God does some spring cleaning for us, it helps to remember that He has our best in mind.

TAKING THE RISK

The heart of man plans his way,
but the LORD establishes his steps.

PROVERBS 16:9

B ack in college, my friends and I went to a career fair. Before attending, I researched the companies I wanted to go see. There was one company I didn't feel good about, but my friend talked me into taking a look at it. On the day of the fair, I went to their booth first. I talked to them about my experience, my major, and what I loved doing. After a few minutes, I said my goodbyes and made sure my resume was one of the firsts on their pile. A day or so later, I received an email requesting another interview. That ended up being my first job out of college. It was perfect and more than I could have ever dreamed of!

I don't know why I had doubts about approaching that company, but I am glad I took the risk. Sometimes we need those nudges from our friends and those close to us to push us out of our comfort zones so that we can live out what God has planned for our lives. If my friend had not done this for me, I would have missed out on a great job.

We can talk ourselves out of so many things, but what if we tried them instead? When we break out and take some risks in life, we never know what God might have in store for us. Even one simple change can lead to many amazing things.

Where do we have the opportunity to take some risks? Perhaps it is getting back out in the dating world or applying for that position that may seem out of reach. Maybe it's connecting with a new friend, or trying out a new recipe, a new church, a new pair of shoes . . . the options are endless. Hope for the best, and consider it a fun new adventure. We will never know unless we try!

GO FOR IT!

Today, think of some things that you've been too afraid to do, and decide to do at least one of them. Break free of the chains that hold you back and move forward into a new direction. You never know the amazing things God has in store for you. Take a chance!

WEIGHING IT OUT

For God gave us a spirit not of fear
but of power and love and self-control.

II TIMOTHY 1:7

Sometimes, when we have a big decision to make and we just don't want to make it, we get stuck where we are. That, too, is a decision. Most of us have probably heard of the old "pros and cons" list. When we're deciding to go for it or not, making a pros and cons list can be helpful. During this exercise, it is helpful to give more weight to those items worth more and less weight to those items that aren't as important.

There is nothing wrong with asking others who know us best for advice, and God can even use these people to help point us in the right direction. Sometimes, however, when we ask others' opinions to make sure our choice is right and they say the opposite of how we believe God is leading us, we can get scared and back away. The best guidance, especially for large decisions, is your gut response.

It is so important to pray while we are weighing things. God wants to guide us in the right direction. Sometimes the decision process requires patience. That's okay. We don't have to act immediately. God will make a way when it's the right time. When we finally feel clear direction from Him, it is time to go for it! As we move forward, we can boldly go in the direction He's leading us in without looking back.

GO FOR IT!

Do you have an important decision to make right now? Pray to God for clarity and to make a way. You may have to tread through uneasy water, but there is hope and peace on the other side. It may take a while to get there, but don't give up!

FOR THE LOVE OF...

For the love of money is a root of all kinds of evils.
It is through this craving that some have
wandered away from the faith
and pierced themselves with many pangs.

I TIMOTHY 6:10

There are so many ways to fill our days. We might fill them with work and family and giving of our time to serve others . . . or something else. Why do we do what we do each day?

That's definitely a huge, loaded, and deep question, so let's take a few minutes to think about it. Okay, maybe some of us came back with several reasons, and that's great too! Were any of those reasons for the love of money?

We all need money to live. We need to pay rent or a mortgage, we need to eat, we need clothing, so we have to obtain money somehow. It's when we let the love of money overshadow our focus for what we're called to do that things can get out of whack.

We're reminded in Matthew 6:24: "No one can serve two masters, for either he will hate the one and love the other, or he will be devoted to the one and despise the other. You cannot serve God and money."

When we focus too much on money, our fear of not having enough makes it difficult to see the whole picture as we are making a decision. It also overshadows what God does for us. He loves us and provides for all of creation faithfully. We are precious to Him. We can trust Him to meet our needs too.

GO FOR IT!

It's a beautiful thing to love what you do each day, and we all should! We have to do a self-check every once in a while and ask ourselves if we are doing it for the love of our paycheck, or to serve God. Let's use our talents, gifts, and purpose for Him.

HOW LIFE CHANGES

For everything there is a season,
and a time for every matter under heaven.

ECCLESIASTES 3:1

Sometimes we get what we prayed for only to find it actually scares us when it happens. I still remember being single and having a place to myself for the first time. I didn't know how to be alone. I found myself in a rut—waking up, getting ready for work, making my lunch, going to work, coming home to eat dinner alone, watch some TV, and go to bed. I longed for a family and a husband, but it wasn't time just yet. Today, ten years later, I could use some alone time now that I have a husband and children. My shower has become my safe haven—or getting up early before anyone else does.

Sometimes, it can scare us when we actually get to the stage of life that we so desperately wanted for so long. We feel unequipped for what this new part of life will bring. Blessings and fear collide.

It is comforting to remember that God walks with us along the way. Often, we learn even as we go, and that's okay too! We don't have to have it all figured out to live out our God-given purposes and what He has planned for us.

Ecclesiastes tells us that there is a season for everything. We are free to enjoy where we are, trusting that God goes with us and that His timing is perfect.

GO FOR IT!

No matter where you are in life today, soak it in. This season may only be a short while, or it may be a long while, but you're here, and you're where you're supposed to be. So sit back, relax, and enjoy the ride. When the seasons start to change, you'll know, and God will equip you along the way!

you
have
a
purpose

YOUR TREASURES

Do not lay up for yourselves treasures on earth,
where moth and rust destroy
and where thieves break in and steal,
but lay up for yourselves treasures in heaven,
where neither moth nor rust destroys
and where thieves do not break in and steal.
For where your treasure is,
there your heart will be also.

MATTHEW 6:19-21

As we boldly live out our God-given purposes and plans for our lives, it helps to occasionally do inward checks to look for anything that is holding us back. What we treasure might hinder us from living out our purposes. According to Scripture, the things we treasure have a lot to say about our hearts. Matthew reminds us that we can't take our possessions with us to heaven. When we have resources, money, and power, we have to be careful not to trust in them. They can be stolen, lost, destroyed, and God reminds us that this isn't where our treasure should be. Our treasures should be stored in heaven, where our heart should be too.

Our hearts should find their treasures in Jesus, who is the greatest treasure. We can follow Him and let our daily pursuits glorify Him. We can use our God-given talents for His glory. These treasures then can be stored in heaven, where nothing can break in and steal and moths cannot destroy.

GO FOR IT!

If you aren't sure where to start, you can begin simply by taking a look inward and seeing if and how you need a change. Instead of living a life of overabundance, we can live generously, giving to those in need with a pure heart and with pure intentions. Check your heart and its desires. What can you do today to redirect your desires so that they honor God?

OWN WORST ENEMY

*The heart is deceitful above all things,
and desperately wicked:
who can know it?*

JEREMIAH 17:9 KJV

We can be our own worst enemies. When we're on a positive pursuit or living out a normal day, negativity can start to creep in and steal our joy. It can also remind us of our own "flaws," which we make so much bigger than they actually are. Before we know it, something small can snowball out of control, completely throwing us off course.

I can't imagine speaking to the people I love the way I speak to myself at times. How would they feel? God loves us and wants us to treat ourselves with kindness and grace. We are God's children, His creation—so why put down something He created?

Perhaps it is critical statements others have said to us that are holding us back. It is easy to let these boil inside, causing much pain, which can go on for years. Let's try to quit being so hard on ourselves. We are beautiful and wonderful creations. If we keep thinking negative thoughts, we might truly become them. No matter what happens today, whether success or failure, let's breathe in and out, and give ourselves some grace.

GO FOR IT!

Today, write down all the things that pop into your head that put yourself down. They can be little things or big things. Include the things you worry about too such as "He doesn't really love me" or "They wouldn't want me to sit with them" and so on. Take a good, long look at these. Where did they originate from? Would people really say that or think that of you? Most likely not. If it's something that is true that you need to work on, this can motivate you to change to be a better person. If it's a lot of negative self-talk, it needs to stop. Instead, write the truth next to each item. For example, if you think you don't look great today, write what you do find that you love about how you look. Start doing this until those thoughts are long gone. Replace the negative thoughts with the real truth and positivity. Remember, you are God's creation, and you are loved just the way you are!

SOUL RESTORATION

The LORD is my shepherd; I shall not want.
He makes me lie down in green pastures.
He leads me beside still waters. He restores my soul.
He leads me in paths of righteousness for his name's sake.

PSALM 23:1-3

There's a Christian song that's based on this passage, and I can hear it in my mind as I write this devotion. These words serve as a great reminder that we can find rest and refuge in Jesus, and allow Him to lead us as a shepherd would. When we come to Him and rely on Him, He can restore our souls.

We often rely too much on our own selves to fix our problems, and we live with anxiety and stress. Psalm 23 reminds us that we don't have to do it all alone. When we feel burdened and weary, we can find peace through Jesus. We can come to Him in prayer, and even by turning on worship music on the radio, we can sing or simply listen to the lyrics to calm down what's troubling our hearts.

When our souls feel the need for restoration, let's remember the rest of Psalm 23: "Even though I walk through the valley of the shadow of death, I will fear no evil, for you are with me; your rod and your staff, they comfort me. You prepare a table before me in the presence of my enemies; you anoint my head with oil; my cup overflows. Surely goodness and mercy shall follow me all the days of my life, and I shall dwell in the house of the LORD forever"(Psalm 23:4–6).

These verses remind us that God lovingly provides for us in all situations. We can learn to relax and trust in our Shepherd.

GO FOR IT!

Close your eyes and visualize what Psalm 23 is saying. Picture a beautiful, sunny day and a beautiful green pasture. The grass is the perfect height, with beautiful wildflowers here and there. Beside the pasture is a lovely, peaceful body of water. Maybe there are a few fish swimming in it ever so gently. This peaceful place in your mind is somewhere that you can come anytime, any day. Jesus is always ready, His hands and heart open, to be our Shepherd and restore our souls.

DIFFICULT TIMES

For I consider that the sufferings
of this present time are not worth comparing
with the glory that is to be revealed to us.

ROMANS 8:18

I just want it to end, I thought to myself each day during our home renovation. There was always something popping up that needed my attention. Renovation never happens the way it does on TV. It can be a long process with many decisions, and for me, this time wasn't joyful. It was full of anxiety. I wanted to run away from it all, but as the walls were torn out and dust settled everywhere, I knew I had to endure it until it was finally finished.

We can often look at something beautiful and think it was always that way. However, beauty can come from ashes. There's the famous saying, "No pain, no gain." Wouldn't it just be nice and easy if gain could happen without all the pain?

There are all kinds of difficult times that happen in life. We often want to run away to make it stop. When we're in the middle of it all, though, there's often no way of turning back. We never want to leave what's hurting us in the moment and put that on someone else. Sure, I could have put my house up for sale and said "Forget it!" right in the middle of the renovation. But, instead, I endured, and in the end, it all paid off.

We often wonder why we go through difficult times. We can use our pain and our story to help another person through similar circumstances. We can turn our ashes into something beautiful. Try to remember that God draws especially near during these times. He doesn't want us to go through them alone. The difficult times may last just a few months, or they may last years on end. When we're in the thick of it, we can cling to God. We can't and shouldn't go through hard times alone. When we feel like running, let's remember to run into the arms of Jesus rather than away from the problem. There can be a way through, because He is a waymaker!

GO FOR IT!

None of us are exempt from difficult times—they're just a part of life. We can choose to let them fill us with sadness, anxiety, worry, and anger, or we can surrender it all to Jesus. We can come to Him in prayer and look to Him for guidance. Jesus can lead us by still waters when the whole world seems to be shaking. Today, no matter what you're going through, He is with you.

LIVING BOLDLY

Therefore, since we have such a hope,
we are very bold.
II CORINTHIANS 3:12 NIV

When we hear the word *bold*, some of us automatically think of people who are outgoing. But we can live boldly even when our personalities are more reserved. Being bold is more than just an action; I'm talking about it being a mentality. Having a bold mentality will help us through challenging times, allowing us to stand firm and not be easily shaken as we depend on God for strength. It also helps us confidently use the talents and strengths God gave us to bless others. Now, that's bold. When others see us live this way, they also may want to know how to have a faith like ours.

When we're called by God to do something, then let's do it, even if it feels scary. One of the biggest things I remember when God was leading me to move was how uneasy I felt and how badly I wanted to stay—because staying was comfortable. It's not often easy, but when we push away what's comfortable to choose what's best for us instead, we can get ourselves out of deep holes before they begin to form. Often the longer we're in a place, situation, or relatonship, the harder it is to obey what God wants us to do.

GO FOR IT!

Today, think about your talents. Those are gifts that you're given to bring light into this world. Boldly use them for God's glory. Remember, we're all unique!

NOT FINISHED YET

Put off your old self,
which belongs to your former manner of life
and is corrupt through deceitful desires,
and . . . be renewed in the spirit of your minds,
and . . . put on the new self,
created after the likeness of God
in true righteousness and holiness.

EPHESIANS 4:22-24

It has often been said that "it's never too late to start." These words hold so much truth. As we get older, we can think that we're too old to start something new or to start over. It's never too late. Often we let the fear of failure creep in instead of thinking of the positive and wonderful things that can happen once we break through that barrier of self-doubt. God isn't finished with us yet!

This is true no matter our circumstances. The options are endless and so is our potential. We can think "never again" for so many things, but I'm here to say that just because a coin flips to heads nine times out of ten, it doesn't mean that it will do it the tenth time. The odds are always 50/50 no matter what. Doubt and deflection can keep us from pursuing things our heart has longed for. Just because things didn't work out before doesn't mean they won't in the future.

If we never try, then we'll never know. Let's resist the impulse to let the fear of failure stop us from starting down a new path. I love hearing stories like the grandma who tried yoga for the first time in her sixties or the man who finally learned how to fish later in life. Life is full of possibilities, no matter your age!

GO FOR IT!

If you feel that you're in a rut, finding a new passion can bring light into your life. What if you pick up an art or photography class, or maybe learn how to ballroom dance? What's holding you back? If you have already been called to do something new, maybe this is your hint that it's time to make a move! Follow God and see what amazing things He has in store for you!

WRONG PATH

But the Helper, the Holy Spirit,
whom the Father will send in my name,
he will teach you all things
and bring to your remembrance
all that I have said to you.

JOHN 14:26

Occasionally we get the sinking feeling that we are on the wrong path in life. It may not be in all areas, but maybe there's that one area where we feel uneasy. We might find ourselves in a situation that no longer serves us, or realize that we are in the right place but the timing is all wrong. Either way, we look around and suddenly realize life isn't going how we expected.

For those who are in that position and wondering how to get back on track, I have good news. As our faith grows, we will learn more about how to hear from God when we need direction. He communicates to us in so many different ways—through others, through the Holy Spirit's promptings, through His Word, and more. We may not hear a booming voice from above, but the Holy Spirit is always there to help guide us each day and each step of the way.

We can rest in the promise that God has a plan for our lives even when we feel like things have gone awry. We all have those times where things just don't feel right or we feel like we're living in the "in-between." There has to be a middle before moving on to the next step. It can feel weird and uncomfortable, but hold strong and be brave through it! Our times of waiting are wise teachers, and fear not—the ride hasn't come to a halt yet. There is new life on the other side.

GO FOR IT!

Most of us will experience a season when we feel uneasy or unsure of the path we're going down. Rest in God's love for you and pray for direction. It may not happen right away, but the path will be ready for you when the time is right. You won't stay on that uneasy path forever—your course can change at any time, and when it does, go for it!

I AM KNOWN

Search me, O God, and know my heart!
Try me and know my thoughts!
And see if there be any grievous way in me,
and lead me in the way everlasting!

PSALM 139:23-24

I t's pretty amazing that even in the times when we don't feel understood by others, we are known and loved by God. Sometimes it's hard to go to someone else with our problems, but God knows what we're struggling with and who we truly are. When we don't know who we can turn to or when we feel like no one understands, God does. Having this peace can help us through the tough times.

When we let leftovers from dinner sit too long on the counter before we put them in the refrigerator, they go bad. The same thing happens when we have something on our minds, hearts, or souls that needs attention. We worry about it, we get anxiety over it, and we let our minds go down dark paths, when instead, we need to bring it into the light and let God help us with it. We might think we're too busy to go to God with what's bothering us, or we think He may not care or understand, but the opposite is true.

GO FOR IT!

One of the best times to talk to God is when you're driving. Often you're in the car alone so it's a great time to get the things off your chest that you don't want to share with others. You can turn down the music and just pour your heart out to Him in prayer with confidence. Getting everything out there in the open is freeing. God knows you so well, so you don't have to feel like you need to hide anything or be scared. He has you in the palm of His hand, and He loves you just the way you are!

BE STILL,
BUT DON'T BE STILL

Be still, and know that I am God.
I will be exalted among the nations,
I will be exalted in the earth!

PSALM 46:10

This Scripture encourages us to just be still and keep our eyes on God when life feels like it is falling apart. We can learn to trust in God in even the most frightening moments and let Him show us what He can do! As we're called to be still in our walk with the Lord, this doesn't mean just sitting back and letting life pass us by because God is taking care of it all. Spoiler alert: We still have to take action. But our hearts, minds, and souls can rest easy by being still and knowing He's in control and has a plan.

And when God says it is time to move, move! I've found that when He's calling me to do something and I don't take action, something is off in my soul. This can often happen when we don't want to make changes. We might even go to our friends so they can talk us into staying in an area of our lives that is causing us much pain and anxiety because that is what is familiar to us. God wants what is best for us, so we can trust the Lord and "go for it" boldly, instead of being timid and unsure.

GO FOR IT!

When life feels out of control, remember that God is walking beside you. Be still in your heart, trusting that He is bigger than whatever trial you are facing. The more you lean into the movement He's making in your life, the easier it is to know when He's changing things up for your good and it is time to move. The stories in the Bible show us that God calls people to do some uneasy things, and eventually, we will experience that too. Today, be reminded to be still, but when it is time to take action, go for it!

work

for it

WINNING TITLE

The LORD is my rock and my fortress
and my deliverer, my God, my rock,
in whom I take refuge, my shield,
and the horn of my salvation, my stronghold.

PSALM 18:2

When I was in the car with my son recently, he told me he likes Daddy's car better because it's faster. I reminded him that faster isn't always the best. My little boy loves to challenge his sister to see who can get ready for bed the fastest or buckle up in the car first. But being first or being the fastest doesn't always mean you're "winning." Often those who are number one have a lot to live up to. They're striving to keep their title while worrying who's gaining on them from behind.

When we try to be number one in our own lives, whether it's at home, work, or in our social groups, it can be draining. We end up feeling guilty when things don't go just right. When we try to overachieve in many directions in life, it can leave us feeling worthless when an area isn't up to par. We compare ourselves to others on social media, looking at one moment of their lives captured in a photo and feeling like we just can't keep up.

When we consider each of our own lives and situations, we realize we can't compare them to another's highlight reel.

But this isn't the only place unhealthy competition can creep in. We also need to be careful about competing with ourselves—adding more expectations and more weight until we end up breaking. This kind of thing can take a toll before we realize it—and the burnout is brutal.

GO FOR IT!

What are you really striving toward? Ask the Lord today how you can have some weight lifted from your shoulders so that you can live without comparison and burnout. Often the goals we have for ourselves can be unreasonable, and we can be our worst enemies. Today, give yourself a pat on the back for everything that you've accomplished. Just know that you don't have to do it all, and when you feel like you're losing pace, lean on God to strengthen you along the way.

BEING ALL IN

I know your works: you are neither cold nor hot.
Would that you were either cold or hot!
So, because you are lukewarm,
and neither hot nor cold,
I will spit you out of my mouth.

REVELATION 3:15-16

Who has been on a roller coaster before? It's certainly an adventure. Some roller coasters are nice and easy, others do a few crazy twists and turns and loops. Either way, we get in our seats and hold on tight (or raise our hands!), understanding that once the ride starts going, we can't get off; we have to stay on it until it is over.

When we choose to go on the ride, we're all in.

This reminds me of what it is like to live a life of faith. Sometimes we buckle in and hold on tight; we let our lives be an adventure as we rely on God to keep us safe through the twists and turns. Other times, we start on the journey and immediately want off. We are afraid because we don't know if God really has everything under control.

When we feel afraid, let's try to remember that life may

throw us terrifying twists and turns, but the Lord is holding us. We can learn to rely on Him through the loops in life.

When we're *all* in in our faith, we can put our hands up. Not only in worship but on this ride of life. Let life be an adventure instead of something consuming you with worry and anxiety. When you let go of control, God's love for you will always hold.

GO FOR IT!

When it comes to your faith, don't be lukewarm. We've all tasted lukewarm water, and when you compare it to a nice, cold beverage or a steaming hot one, it just doesn't measure up! God doesn't want you to be unsure; He wants you to trust Him along the ride of your life. Consider your life and faith journey an adventure! God's got you as you go through all the crazy twists and turns. Sometimes you can't see what's up ahead, but instead of letting it give you anxiety and worry, enjoy the ride!

BUSY DOESN'T EQUAL WORTH

For by grace you have been saved through faith.
And this is not your own doing;
it is the gift of God, not a result of works,
so that no one may boast.

EPHESIANS 2:8-9

We live in a hurry-up world. If we don't keep up, we fall behind. We often associate busyness and productivity with our worth. I have had this perspective on worth much of my life, especially in college. I felt like if I wasn't busy or productive with classwork, I didn't know what to do with myself. I let life pass me by as I put my worth in my time spent working and studying. Today, I still struggle with this tendency with my job.

When finding our worth in what we do each day makes it hard for us to rest, we find ourselves drained and defeated. We shouldn't associate worthiness with doing good work. Our worth shouldn't be defined by putting checkmarks in our planners. So what is it all for? We're reminded that ultimately, our work is for the Lord. Check this out in

Colossians 3:17: "And whatever you do, in word or deed, do everything in the name of the Lord Jesus, giving thanks to God the Father through him."

Our work is meant to glorify God, and our worth is found in Him alone. So work joyfully, but also rest deeply when you need it. You are more than what you do!

GO FOR IT!

If you associate your worth with your busyness, you can find yourself defeated and exhausted. You can't earn your worth. It was given to you as a gift through God's love for you. If you're struggling with finding your worth or realizing it was in the wrong place, know that you can find it in Jesus. You are worthy!

PREPARING A WAY

It is the LORD who goes before you.
He will be with you;
he will not leave you or forsake you.
Do not fear or be dismayed.

DEUTERONOMY 31:8

There are a lot of new housing developments in the city where I live. Trees are being torn down and land cleared for new homes. What was once farmland or forest is being transformed into something completely different.

God does this with us too. While we are busy living out our day to day, He goes before us and prepares a way. He lays the foundation and groundwork for our lives, and when it's the right time, He moves us.

Deuteronomy 31:8 is such a good reminder that we don't have to walk this life alone. God is the same today as He ever was and ever will be. He goes with us throughout our life journeys and will never leave or forsake us!

Sometimes it's hard to look at a forest or farmland and picture what it would look like developed. We can look at each of our lives the same way. A plan is laid out for us and carried through, but we may not see what God's preparing for us until it is finished. We can trust that God has made a way, and He's just preparing us for it!

GO FOR IT!

When you look at each day, if often seems the same as the rest. But as you look back over the years, wow, things have changed, right? Sometimes God puts you in certain situations to prepare you for what He has planned for your future. He's building something for you that you just don't see yet. When you feel like your life is changing, don't be worried or afraid. He's with you through it all, and He is preparing you for what's ahead.

CONSUMING THOUGHTS

*He went on a little farther
and got down with His face on the ground.
He prayed, "My Father, if it can be done,
take away what is before Me.
Even so, not what I want but what You want."*

MATTHEW 26:39 NLV

It is easy to let our thoughts consume us day after day. Some of us struggle with the same worry or anxiety over and over. One way we can deal with these thoughts is to write them all down in a journal. It helps to find a quiet spot or maybe turn on some music in the background as we talk to God about what's on our minds. We can think of it as a conversation, like He's sitting right beside us.

We can ask God to help us sort everything out and rely on our faith to bring us through it. When we submit these things to the Lord, they can't take our minds, bodies, and souls captive anymore. When anxious thoughts start creeping back into our minds, let's remind ourselves that we've already given it to God to handle for us.

GO FOR IT!

Let God be strong for you when you are weak. When Jesus prayed in Matthew 26:39, He ended it with "Even so, not what I want but what You want" (NLV). That is faith. Faith isn't waiting for God to move as we'd like Him to, but according to His will. Today, try bringing your troubles to Him. He wants to hear from you! Let Him replace your worry and stress with His grace and love instead.

PREPARING FOR BATTLE

Put on the whole armor of God,
that you may be able to stand
against the schemes of the devil.

EPHESIANS 6:11

Each day is a battle for every single one of us, whether we see it or not. Evil forces can prey on our weaknesses and cause much tribulation in our souls. They can make us question whether God is for us or not and make us believe false things about Him, ourselves, and others. We are called to put on the whole armor of God, His truth, His goodness, and His peace, to stand against these attacks.

Our souls are so precious. Sometimes we unknowingly succumb to the negativity around us. Each day, we have to prepare to resist it. As we notice critical or judgmental thoughts creeping into our minds or words tearing us or someone else down—let's stop and remind ourselves of God's love and truth. With God's help, we can turn away from these harmful thoughts and learn to acknowledge them as they arise!

GO FOR IT!

Each day, it's important to stay close to God. You can put on the armor of God any time of the day or anytime you feel you're under attack. The truth of who God is can help you in the storms, as well as His goodness and peace. When you're feeling attacked, let your faith be your shield and don't let those thoughts enter your mind. Be bold and unafraid to stand strong in your faith!

TRIALS TO TESTIMONY

He said to them, "Go into all the world
and proclaim the gospel to the whole creation."

MARK 16:15

Have you ever shared your faith with someone? As we learned in Mark 16:15, we're called to share about Jesus so that others may learn the good news of His love.

Sometimes we hesitate to talk about our faith because we're too scared that we'll come off the wrong way and push others away. But what if our story helps bring another to the Lord?

My story began when I was little. We went to a traditional-style church occasionally, but I didn't get much out of it. Since our attendance was spotty, I felt out of place in kids' church since I didn't know the other kids and felt like everyone else was a "regular." It wasn't until I was in eighth grade and had gone through confirmation at my church that I really felt God calling me into a deeper relationship with Him. It came at just the right time, too, because that summer I lost all of the friends I knew before going into high school. I was cyberbullied, and I felt alone and afraid.

God had a bigger plan, though. I began using my Bible I got during confirmation. Each night, I would open it randomly to a page that ended up being just what I needed to hear. God pulled me through that difficult time and made me stronger in my faith.

Now looking back, I'm so glad I wasn't friends with those girls going into high school. God pulled me away from them for a reason, to have the friend group I was meant to have. It is difficult to see it in the middle of hard times, but God provides a way, even when there is no way. I'll never forget a greeting card my grandma gave me that had Jeremiah 29:11 on the front to help me through those rough days. I still have that card today.

GO FOR IT!

When I was in the middle of it, I didn't realize that my lonely season just before high school was a pivotal moment in my faith journey. Since then, I've discovered that God has always been there for me, through good times and bad.

God brought good out of those terrible times. Now, I thank Him for taking some relationships and jobs out of my life that weren't meant for me anymore. I hope this helps you too in your journey. Don't be afraid; share your story! You never know who needs to hear it!

WANT WHAT HE WANTS

My son, give me your heart,
and let your eyes observe my ways.

PROVERBS 23:26

Surrender is hard. We like to be in control of so much of our lives, and when we don't get what we want when we want it, we get upset. But, just as a good father wants his son to listen to his guidance, God wants us to keep our hearts tender to His leading.

Sometimes we begin to resist God's leading because we are struggling to trust that He knows what is best for us. Like a rebellious son, we pull away from God's love. But having faith is more than just going to church, it's believing and trusting in something we just can't see. After all, we can't see "love" in our lives, but it's there

No problem is ever too big for God to handle. When we surrender what we're carrying and allow Him to guide us, our heavy hearts become light.

When we let God lead, we are in the best hands. He sees all and has our best interests in mind.

GO FOR IT!

What's standing in your way today that's stopping you from surrendering to what God wants for your life? It can be hard to give up that control, but once you do, your faith and relationship with Jesus will be forever changed. Today, pray for God to show you how to surrender to what He wants for you!

BEARING FRUIT

But the fruit of the Spirit is love, joy, peace, patience, kindness, goodness, faithfulness, gentleness, self-control; against such things there is no law.

GALATIANS 5:22-23

I'm sure you can think of a time when you met someone who was a true delight—someone patient and joyful, kind and gentle, and who showed great love no matter what they were doing. Galatians 5:22–23 tells us that these characteristics, along with four others—peace, goodness, faithfulness, and self-control—are the "fruit of the Spirit." These fruits are the result of God's work in our lives when we are obedient to the His Spirit. They are not the fruit of our own strength, but of God's strength within us. In fact, if we tried to develop these characteristics on our own strength and determination, we would fall short by comparison. However, if we have accepted God as our Lord and Savior, we have the power of the Spirit working in us right now— and He is changing us day by day.

Sometimes it seems like there's a dark cloud hanging over your heads. It can be hard to sense His Spirit on those days. Try closing your eyes and facing the sun and inviting His Spirit to fill you completely. And then be still, take your time, let His gentleness consume you. The Holy Spirit is one of God's most precious gifts to His beloved children.

GO FOR IT!

When our lives are filled with the Holy Spirit, others will see Jesus through us, by how we live. But the fruit of the Spirit is a blessing to our lives too. We can go to God and ask Him to fill us with love, joy, and peace. We are worth it!

good
things
take
time

THE POWER OF PATIENCE

But if we hope for what we do not yet have,
we wait for it patiently.

ROMANS 8:25 NIV

Having patience with others can be tough, really tough, especially when you have a lot going on at home or at work. Sometimes it's best to take a deep breath and say a prayer before reacting to the long line at the pharmacy, or the eight miles of bumper-to-bumper traffic on the interstate, or the child who just made the same mistake for the one hundredth time. My patience wears thin when trying to get my kids to school on time. I always feel rushed and the morning never goes as planned, and before I know it, I'm frustrated. But there are ways around getting myself into this fix. Maybe getting up earlier could help me calm the chaos that surrounds our current morning routine.

But how is patience developed as a characteristic of who we are at our cores? How can we walk through life with a loving patience that never goes away? Well, first we need to cooperate with the Holy Spirit who is developing patience in us (and we do this by obeying and abiding in

Him). And we can always look at the ultimate example of a patient man—Jesus Christ. There are countless accounts of Him showing patience throughout His time on earth. He was patient with His disciples, despite their lack of faith and their slowness to understand His divine mission. He was patient with the crowds, with those who reached out for His healing power, and with little children.

Christ is our perfect model, and the more we become like Him, the more we will have patience: with our families, our friends, our coworkers, the people in traffic, and even ourselves.

GO FOR IT!

When you hit a bump on your path that causes frustration, don't be alarmed. And don't let the bump stop you from continuing the bike ride. In some cases, trials can produce patience. James 1:2–3 ICB says, "You will have many kinds of troubles. But when these things happen, you should be very happy. You know that these things are testing your faith. And this will give you patience."

DILIGENT FAITH

The soul of the sluggard craves and gets nothing,
while the soul of the diligent is richly supplied.

PROVERBS 13:4

Sometimes we find ourselves feeling like we've gotten into a rut. Things aren't terrible, exactly, but they aren't great either. This is interesting to think about as we read Proverbs 13:4 as it contrasts the life of a "sluggard" with that of a "diligent" person. The word "diligence" means to pay attention to something, to show that we care. When we get into these ruts, situations in which it seems we "get nothing," the way out is through diligence. Let's dive into some areas where we can bring some new life to the mundane.

If our romantic relationships are in a rut, it might help to ask ourselves if we are speaking our partners' "love languages." How do they like to receive love? Do they like to have love notes, a back rub, their lunch made for them, or even the house and dishes cleaned up for them? Maybe it's just saying the simple "I love you!" more often or giving them a good, long hug.

What about our friendships? A simple text or phone call can go a long way. If we have friends who are going through a hard time, we might ask them how we can help. A hot meal or simple surprise on their doorstep may just make their day! When we truly care for others, we're living like Jesus. He found the suffering and made them feel loved when they didn't feel loved.

Whether we work inside or outside of the house, it is easy to get in a rut, and diligence is the way out. If it's at work, how can we go the extra mile? Digging deeper and running an extra report or showing extra care can go a long way and make a manager sit up and take notice. At home, what are some areas where we can be more diligent? Maybe it's going through some piles we've been putting off, donating unused clothes or items, or doing that deep clean we have been procrastinating.

GO FOR IT!

You have the power to affect the lives of others in a positive way by caring for them. Doing something for someone else can help bring you joy too! Today, think of how you can live more like Jesus and show others some love!

GAINING CONFIDENCE

*For the Spirit God gave us does not make us timid,
but gives us power, love and self-discipline.*

II TIMOTHY 1:7 NIV

Some of us are more confident than others, but how about gaining confidence in the Lord? Jesus is and was confident, not arrogant. There is a big difference, but it's important to recognize that we can be one, not the other. As we lay down our own plans and pick up what God has for us instead, we need to be confident in our faith walk with the Lord to see us through. We can have confidence in God's plans for us!

God's work is never finished in us. He won't say, "Here's your life" and then leave us. Let's remain faithful and be confident that He's got us! We're reminded in 1 John 3:20–21 to have confidence before God, and He is greater than our heart! He knows our hearts—He knows everything!

God wants to have a relationship with us. He will seek us, and He wants us to come to Him with everything—our cares, dreams, desires, and needs. He wants us to bring all of those burdens to Him. As we give these up, we can have confidence that God will take care of them all, for His glory and in His timing!

We are not called to boast in arrogance, but we can share this great news with others: God is with us, He is for us, and He will never forsake us.

GO FOR IT!

As you boldly live out God's plans for you, stay confident in your walk with the Lord. You can come to Him anytime, for anything. He hears all of your prayers and cries and knows your deepest desires and struggles. As you build your confidence in the Lord, others will be able to see this through you and want to know more about the hope you have found in Jesus.

LOVING THE UNLOVABLE

Owe no one anything, except to love each other,
for the one who loves another has fulfilled the law.

ROMANS 13:8

I love you, Mommy!" my daughter said to me the other day.

"I love you too, Kenleigh!" I said back.

"I love Daddy and Jackson and EVERYBODY!" she exclaimed.

I laughed and said, "That's good!"

To her, everyone is her best friend, and her innocence is precious.

It isn't so easy to love the people who have hurt us. The Bible talks a lot about loving one another. I think about the stories in which Jesus went to those who were "unlovable"—the tax collector, the leper, the prostitute . . . . He went out of His way to spend time with people that others passed by. He knew they desperately needed to feel real love.

We can show love to others in countless ways. We're called to love the oppressed and extend a hand toward them, just as Jesus did, remembering that we are all made in the image of God. Even those that have a hardened heart or those that have hurt us need love.

How can we show these people love? We can pray for them, that their hearts would be softened and for relationships to be restored. We don't know what is going on in their minds, hearts, and souls. They too could have been hurt by someone in their past, and the snowball effect makes us the next victim. Love is the only way to break the cycle of hurt.

GO FOR IT!

Loving these people starts with forgiveness. We have to give the hurt to Jesus and forgive them in our hearts, minds, and souls. We aren't meant to live with the hurt forever. Give it to God, trusting Him with the outcome.

HOW FAR YOU'VE COME

Now faith is the assurance of things hoped for,
the conviction of things not seen.

HEBREWS 11:1

Let's take a few moments to just look around and see how far we've come. As we do, we might remember the trials and tribulations, the peaks and valleys. We might think of our family situations, our jobs, or our deepest desires that we have brought to God in prayer. God is working in our lives. Sometimes we get so busy living that we don't notice how much He has done for us. As we take a look back over our lives, can we see how God worked through different situations to get us where we are today? Maybe He had us meet a certain friend who connected us somehow to the next part of our life. Or maybe He had us miss out on one thing but something greater happened because of it. There are countless ways He worked through it all for our blessing and for His glory.

Let's take this moment to appreciate where we are at this time, right now, and praise Him for what He's done so far in our lives! Storms don't last forever, and we need the rain to grow and thrive. We often think of storms in a negative way, but there is so much beauty that can come from the rain! Without it, we wouldn't have food, green grass, or beautiful flowers. The same is true in our lives!

GO FOR IT!

When you think of your accomplishments, no matter how big or small, thank the Lord for them, as it's all because of Him that you got where you are. You may have a long way to go, but celebrate the small victories along the way. Remember, God's timing is perfect!

LIVING HONESTLY

Then God said, "Let us make man in our image,
after our likeness. And let them have dominion
over the fish of the sea and over the birds of the heavens
and over the livestock and over all the earth
and over every creeping thing that creeps on the earth."

GENESIS 1:26

Recently, my friend posted some truth on social media. She mentioned the things she was showing to others through words and photos—lots of smiles, family, and traveling, yet inside she was struggling. Then, she bravely chose to reveal those struggles in her post. We often look at others and think they have it all together, but we are all going through struggles others don't see, and unless we bring it all into the light, they never will.

We do this with ourselves too. We can tell ourselves that we're okay when we're not, but it is so liberating to live honestly. When we know God loves us just as we are, we are free to choose authenticity versus trying to be what we want others to think of us.

Many people fear being authentic—that if others see the truth, they won't be accepted or loved. When we are confident of Jesus' love for us, we are free to stop pretending. Each of us is beautiful, wonderfully made in the image of God. There will never be anyone like us ever again, and never has there been before.

God loves us. When we know Who's got us, and Whose we are, we can face anything.

GO FOR IT!

To begin living honestly, start by loving who you truly are! Accept yourself and how you were made—flaws and all. We can be so hard on ourselves, but it's time to show the world the real you—the mess and all! No matter what, remember that God loves you, just as you are.

WITH AND WITHOUT

Though he brings grief, he will show compassion,
so great is his unfailing love. For he does not willingly
bring affliction or grief to anyone.

LAMENTATIONS 3:32-33 NIV

A while back, I got together with one of my friends. She called and told me she had exciting news and wanted to meet up. I was pregnant and was so excited to see her. We talked about life, work, and everything in between. Then the words and tears came—between the time we had scheduled the lunch and when we finally got together, her exciting news had turned to heartbreak. She had had a miscarriage. Here I was, happily pregnant, hearing of her sorrow. My heart felt terrible. I was with, and she was without. There were no words I could say to perfectly console her pain. She wanted to get together to tell me they were pregnant, and then as we got together, the little one was lost. I felt her pain, deeply. This wasn't the first time a friend had let me know this had happened. I have had friends suffer miscarriages and also friends going through infertility. Each of their stories has been heartbreaking. Often it's hard to understand where God is in these moments.

I have also been on the other side of "with and without." Before my marriage, I worried that I'd always be a bridesmaid, never a bride. My friends were getting married and were *with*, while I was *without*. Eventually, I started to make my own life without having someone by my side, trusting that God's plan was best. Still, my season of "without" was painful.

It can be hard to be happy for someone when you're on the painful side of "with and without." Now that I've been on both sides, I've learned a few things. First, no words can take away any pain perfectly, only Jesus can do that. It's okay to cry, but instead of getting mad and running from God, we must run toward Him. He will hold us through it all.

We can also seek others who will surround us with love and care. This is how Jesus' love works its way out in the world, through the way we love each other.

We may never understand why we go through loss, but we can still boldly live out the plans God has for us. We can be confident in our faith, even when it's hard to hold on to anything else.

GO FOR IT!

When we are *with*, how can we give to those *without*? This can be for so many situations—those without shelter, food, love, a relationship, a baby . . . and more. When you give of your time, resources, and prayer, it may not solve all the problems, but it will certainly help. Being there for your friends when they are hurting them shows much love!

COMING IN PRAYER

Pray without ceasing.

I THESSALONIANS 5:17

Growing up, I would say the same prayer before bed each night, and let's be honest, I still do! I even taught my kids the same prayer and they say it before bed. Some families pray before each meal, while others do so just at dinner or only on holidays. Some people pray while they're driving or having quiet time with the Lord. There is no one right way to pray. What's important is that God loves hearing from you!

He also loves to hear your praise. We can praise Him for all He's given us. We can praise Him in good times and bad. We can praise Him for His kind and generous heart when we remember that He has given us all things—food, shelter, water, and sunshine. Remember, He is our Father God. As children, we may not always understand Him, but we can still obey and trust our Father God.

We can share His love with the world by praying for others. We can ask God to meet their needs and comfort them when they are hurting. We can pray for those who have hurt us, and ask God to give us forgiving hearts.

God wants us to come to Him with what's on our hearts. He's there to listen. We don't have to limit our prayers to just morning or bedtime. We can pray when we have quiet time or when we are alone. Even using Christian music to sing to God in worship and in prayer can be a whole new way to pray.

GO FOR IT!

Today, take your time in prayer. There is no need to be anxious, there is no "right" way to pray. God won't judge you. He loves you! Try incorporating these various ways of praying mentioned in today's devotion into your daily routine for a few days and see how you feel. I pray your relationship with the Lord grows!

GO FOR IT!

And Jesus came and said to them, "All authority
in heaven and on earth has been given to me.
Go therefore and make disciples of all nations,
baptizing them in the name of the Father
and of the Son and of the Holy Spirit,
teaching them to observe all that I have commanded you.
And behold, I am with you always, to the end of the age."

MATTHEW 28:18-20

We made it! The last devotion in *Go For It!* We've touched on so many topics, but one thing remains the same: God's plan for our lives is the best plan. As we live our lives, we can walk in the light of Jesus, knowing that no matter what comes, God is always by our sides and will never leave us! When we wake up in the morning and go to bed each night, we can thank God for His blessings and for hearing our prayers.

Let's live boldly for Him. As we surrender our plans to Him and grow in our faith, we will stay grounded in our faith and in the truth, even when faced with adversity. He's working in and through all things for all of us! As we walk with Jesus, others will see His light shine.

Jesus reminds us in Matthew 28:18–20 that He's always with us, even to the very end. What a comfort to know that He walks with us through all the seasons and storms of life. When we don't know where to turn, we know that we can always turn to Him. This assurance frees us to live our lives as an adventure! There is no limit to what God can do when we say "yes" to the callings He has for us. We never know the wonderful things He has in store! Let's be brave and be bold and just go for it!

GO FOR IT!

I hope today that you surrender your plans, hopes, dreams, *all of it* over to Jesus. In return, know that God's plan for your life is beautiful, even when times are hard. As you journey through this life with Him, share your story with others. Who knows what might happen next? Go for it!

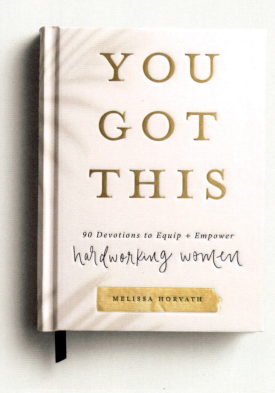

WANT MORE FROM MELISSA?

You can find her devotional You Got This
on dayspring.com, as well as retail stores near you.

ABOUT THE AUTHOR

Melissa Horvath began Sweet Water Decor in her basement in 2014; nine months later, she was working her business full-time. She encourages through her home decor products, well-chosen words, and unique hand lettering. She's been featured in countless publications and networks, was one of Amazon's Women-Owned Businesses to watch in 2018, and resides in Pennsylvania with her husband and three children.

Dear Friend,

      This book was prayerfully crafted with you, the reader, in mind. Every word, every sentence, every page was thoughtfully written, designed, and packaged to encourage you—right where you are this very moment. At DaySpring, our vision is to see every person experience the life-changing message of God's love. So, as we worked through rough drafts, design changes, edits, and details, we prayed for you to deeply experience His unfailing love, indescribable peace, and pure joy. It is our sincere hope that through these Truth-filled pages your heart will be blessed, knowing that God cares about you—your desires and disappointments, your challenges and dreams.

He knows. He cares. He loves you unconditionally.

BLESSINGS!
THE DAYSPRING BOOK TEAM

**Additional copies of this book and
other DaySpring titles can be purchased
at fine retailers everywhere.
Order online at <u>dayspring.com</u>
or
by phone at 1-877-751-4347**